Why Friends Are Friends

Some Quaker Core Convictions

By Jack L. Willcuts

Friends missionary, pastor, superintendent, and
magazine editor

BARC
Nev

Why Friends Are Friends

Copyright © 1984 by Barclay Press

International Standard Book Number: 0-913342-45-9
Library of Congress Catalog Card Number: 84-231509

Cover design by Michael Comfort

Drawings of hands by Jannelle Loewen

Second Printing, 1987
Third printing, 1992
Fourth printing, 2000
Fifth printing, 2002

CONTENTS

*Dedicated to
new Friends
and
young pastors*

FOREWORD

In 1999 Johan Maurer, then general secretary of Friends United Meeting and the speaker at Northwest Yearly Meting sessions, was asked, "Is 'Quaker heritage' a blessing or a curse?" He responded:

> It is a mixed blessing. Quaker faith and practice is to me nothing more or less than a way of Christian discipleship—a way that a particular group of believers have responded to conversion and its ethical requirements, and the ways they have passed on these responses to us as teachings and models. (NWYM *Connection,* Summer 1999)

Johan went on to warn against undue pride in Friends tradition, which he said could degenerate into "a false specialness, a poisonous elitism, when we take out the teaching value and just focus on quakerishness."

Had he lived to hear these words from Johan, Jack Willcuts would definitely have agreed. Jack was intensely loyal to the Friends Church and this book is a call to greater respect and appreciation for its teachings. But Jack very much agreed that believers are to be loyal primarily to Jesus Christ. We don't worship the church; it is only a means through which worship, evangelism, fellowship, and discipleship are provided.

It was my privilege to know Jack as pastor, employer, church leader, and dear friend. He spoke and wrote with passion and clarity, but never gave the impression of being impressed with his own gifts and accomplishments. He was both lighthearted and intense; witty and serious.

After Jack's death in 1989, I wrote a tribute in *Evangelical Friend*, the magazine he had edited for 18 years. The editorial concluded with these words: "Jack, you made such an enormous contribution to the Kingdom of God, particularly in the Friends Church. We're grateful. We can't match the work you've done. We can only determine to continue it with a little of the energy, vision, and persistence you brought to everything you did."

One of Jack's many gifts was the willingness and ability to step across the boundaries between Friends groups. Jack was able to explain his convictions as an evangelical Friend to Quakers who wouldn't call themselves evangelical, but were impressed with the authenticity of Jack's faith and life. Jack spoke of his love for Jesus and reminded his listeners that this was in its essence what turned George Fox from spiritual lostness to spiritual passion.

If Jack were alive today, he would note with appreciation that some of the fear and distrust between Friends groups has diminished. There was a time when the general secretary of FUM would not have been invited to speak at Northwest Yearly Meeting. But if Jack had been on the planning committee in 1999, he would have been one of the first to support the invitation to Johan Maurer, a Friend who knows Jesus and understands what really matters about Friends convictions.

This book invites us to figure out what really matters for Quakers and does so in a positive, biblically sound way. It's too easy to define a movement by what it doesn't practice or believe. Jack was not content to define the Friends movement by the elements of Protestantism that seem to be missing. He wants readers to understand and treasure the positive insights and contributions of Friends and to shape their loyalty to the movement around that insight.

—Lon Fendall
Newberg, Oregon
June 2000

PREFACE

Walking along the Oregon coast at the water's edge, the beauty, the immensity, the majesty of the ocean is impressive. But to understand the ocean, study, respect, and use it as well as admire it takes more than simply walking along the beach. Oceanography is a science. Men across the centuries have made maps of it, charted the tides, analyzed its depth, distances, and dangers. Those who know the sea respect it most and are drawn to its unfathomable strength and beauty.

So with the church. "Theology is the queen of sciences." We do well to respect the depth, history, and majesty of this living creation of God's hand, the church. Quaker Christian convictions are time-tested through faith and practice. Three and a half centuries is quite a while. Early Friends did not attempt to introduce some new and different religion to the world. Nor do we. Walking alongside the tides of time and history, they, and we, make a rediscovery of basic Christianity. Friends have been drawn to the church's unfathomable strength and beauty by faith, a faith shared often at personal peril.

George Fox, "the first instrument" (Penn) of the Society of Friends, was 23 years old when he found personal salvation and peace of mind through Jesus Christ in 1647, after four years of spiritual seeking. He soon became a mighty preacher and leader with a positive Christian message. The Friends rapidly grew in numbers, in spite of severe persecution. They became both evangelists and missionaries. They fervently believed that seventeenth century followers of Christ were to live in the same spirit and power in which the first century Christians lived.

Christian faith and practice in any period should be examined and experienced in the light of the Gospel, centered in Jesus Christ, our Lord, as revealed in the Holy Scriptures and by the Holy Spirit. How these convictions are expressed in personal, practical, relevant ways is the primary reason for this brief attempt to connect our Quaker past with our present and the challenges of our future. These connections become again our own convictions as we return to the revealed Word and the leadings of the Spirit. This is why Friends are Friends.

The subjects selected in this small book are shared because they have shaped the lives of those who belong to Friends. It is important to know why one belongs. Some belong without really knowing why; others leave the Friends Church for similar shallow reasons. The core convictions considered here are not merely some doctrines we hold. They hold us! Without a reasonable faith and inner convincement of Truth, is to simply walk casually along the beaches of a denomination without understanding its beauty, depth, or the dangers when the church is not respected. Those who know the Lord best respect the church most.

The concern for writing this comes partially from sensing the search of several who appear to consider church connections quite casually. Another concern, more intimately personal, comes from lengthy conversations with our own children, who with their families have lived several years where Friends churches are not available. Their doctrinal roots were discovered to be deeper than they had realized. One daughter, Susan Kendall, is in seminary graduate studies and has assisted in the preparation of this manuscript. Our other daughter, Jan Loewen, an artist, has drawn the hands illustrating the different attitudes expressing Friends convictions.

We all need a "church home." This generation faces numerous challenges to faith as well as incredible uncertainties. The advance of technology has contributed an authority that seems real, especially to younger people. Living as we do now on the new edges of knowledge in the fields of medicine, the media, "high tech," space travel, and warfare weaponry produces a feeling of isolation and confusion. We are daily face to face with the potential of intervening variables of nuclear war, hunger, poverty, overpopulation, dwindling resources, and economic uncertainty. Clearly, a new intensity of concern motivates us to find core convictions that are accurate and eternal to match the confusion around us.

—Jack L. Willcuts
January 1984

Chapter I

THE WONDER OF WORSHIP

*"Do not come any closer," God said [to Moses at the burning bush].
"Take off your sandals, for the place where
you are standing is holy ground." —Exodus 3:5 NIV*

What is worship? When that word is used, what comes first to your mind? Something from the Bible, something from childhood, or last Sunday morning?

Does it really matter? I think so. I believe God thinks so. That is the reason so much space is given to it in Scripture. The very first thing God said to Moses in that burning bush incident was, "Take off your shoes!" This is worship, you and Me together...from now on this will be your center of life, your source of information for leadership and wisdom for making all kinds of decisions.

The same could be said again to us. We need some "holy ground," a place, a way, a reality, to verify that God is near and that we want Him near.

Worship. The idea and word means so many different things to different people. It became synonymous with tabernacles, temples, and high priests. In getting our religion straightened out, Jesus also redefined and redesigned worship. It happened

1

when He shouted from the cross, "It is finished!" And down-town the temple veil shielding the "holy of holies" room mirac-ulously ripped from "top to bottom." Not that people could now step inside to examine (or admire) a beautiful room; rather, God stepped outside and into our hearts. "Don't you know that you yourselves are God's temple and that God's Spirit lives in you?" Paul was writing to Christians (1 Cor. 3:16 NIV), telling us the new and correct way to approach worship. He adds something else that makes this whole subject at once majestic and scary: "...God's temple is sacred, and you are that temple." (v. 17)

With that, we see it is only proper to reverently tiptoe through this matter of worship. It isn't as though we can sort over personal tastes and worship denominational styles as one would pick over merchandise at K-Mart.

Nor does worship just happen. Strolling sleepily, or hur-riedly, into a meeting for worship, already bored or duty bound, isn't going to do it—no matter what the ads or printed bulletins say. The disturbing part is how routine and com-monplace that is! Ezekiel observed the same situation and exclaimed: "As surely as I live, declares the Sovereign Lord, because you have defiled my sanctuary with...detestable prac-tices, I myself will withdraw my favor...." (Ezek. 5:11 NIV) Now that *we* are sanctuary hasn't changed the holiness and expec-tations of God.

There are, of course, almost as many ways to worship as there are Christians. There are private devotions, meditation on a mountain somewhere, or at the seaside, family worship at the breakfast table, kneeling at the bedside. There is formal and informal, high and low worship, programmed and unpro-grammed. Worship as communion will be considered later. In Spanish a word for worship is *adoración*. A Hebrew meaning for *worship* is "bowing down." A New Testament word for wor-ship stretches the definition specifically meaning "to serve."

Charles Colson writes of an observation made while he was in the Nixon White House. "What is it about us that caus-es us to withhold from God the reverence we lavish on human idols? Over and over in the White House, I met people who would fiercely complain about a policy and demand an audience with the President. But the roaring lions I escorted from the waiting room became meek lambs in the Oval Office. I saw more awe in that one room than I have seen in the sanctuaries of all our churches combined."

So, now let's step inside the buildings and the rooms of our minds in our worshiping experiences.

"To worship is to experience reality, to touch Life," Richard Foster observes in *Celebration of Discipline*. "It is to know, to feel, to experience the resurrected Christ in the midst of the gathered community."

It isn't as though we have to push or maneuver our way into a worship contact. It brings startling confidence to discover God is "seeking," searching, waiting, longing; He is already there to be with us in a shared worship experience. Jesus said so. "The true worshipers will worship the Father in spirit and truth, for such the Father seeks to worship him." (John 4:23 RSV) It is our response to God's initiative. The only reluctance is ours.

Trendy interests come and go in churches. That worship is currently featured in so many Christian books and magazines now doesn't mean it is just another fad. It is an ongoing, basic, core concept for all that Christianity is. Out of true worship springs all the blessings and service. Without real worship, churches grow stale and boring. Disunity, fruitlessness, *any* problem you can name implies worship dysfunction. Probing at the worship of the church is to be close to the nerve center, the lifeline of spiritual vitality and health.

Worship is a verb, sometimes, as well as a noun. It can be something we *do*, Kierkegaard insists. So, worship is also learned, practiced, and the product of devotional discipline. Leaving worship one should ask, "Lord, how did I do?" rather than, "Did I get anything out of that?"

"Thou shalt have no other gods before me" is the first commandment. That priority is not accidental in the ten listed. It is still number one. A problem is that idols nowadays are so often simply *us*. What do *I* get out of church or worship? How do *I* feel? Are *my* needs being met? It makes all the difference in the world what the object of our worship is. It may be as unfortunate, and sinful, to focus on ourselves or some totally erroneous idea at the center of our worship as it might be to make idols of carved wood or sculptured stone.

While worship is spiritual, it still has structure. There are nuts and bolts to worship planning. Spontaneity in worship, real worship, is a myth. Unplanned, poorly prepared worship can be a bumbling, embarrassing, miserable thing. Even "unprogrammed" meetings require guidelines. Ours is a God of order, and preparation for worship is terribly important!

A striking feature of Old Testament and early church worship was what one might call a "holy expectancy." It is a response to the living Presence. "Worship is the adoring response of the heart and mind to the influence of the Spirit of God." This comes from a Quaker *Discipline* book. "It stands neither in forms nor in the formal disuse of forms; it may be without words as well as with them, but it must be in spirit and in truth."

Describing the worshiping church, D. Elton Trueblood insists it is the "...fellowship of consciously inadequate persons who gather because they are weak. And scatter to serve because their unity one with another and with Christ has made them bold." (*The Incendiary Fellowship*, Harper & Row, 1961, p. 31)

To fail to see past the humanness of the worship hour, to miss the divine-human encounter is not a new problem. The earliest Christians as well as the Old Testament worshipers were warned about the importance of preparation for worship. The "expectancy" was preceded by reverence, and appropriate conduct.

Paul wrote the Corinthian Christians, "...it seems that your church meetings do you more harm than good!" He goes on, "It is this careless participation which is the reason for the many feeble and sickly Christians in your church, and the explanation of the fact that many of you are spiritually asleep." (1 Cor. 11:17, 30 *Phillips*)

What if Paul (or George Fox) were to visit a typical meeting for worship now in one of our local churches? Of course, the Lord is already doing so, but perhaps unnoticed, which is worse... or more wonderful! These rather lofty descriptions and definitions would not mean a lot. The mood, the sense of awe, deepest fulfillment of joy, new insights with hearts that see, these are the characteristics, the sacred stuff of morning worship when God is present.

The size of the church or its membership, the style of the leadership, the choice and performance of songs and singing, all these are not the real reason for good or poor worship. Worship is within. It is a discipline of concentration, remembering, and application; it is not an hour at a service, it is an attitude, a response, a confrontation. It is being with God, then returning to life to serve because we have worshiped. This change of focused attention and direction upward and inward is where knowing God is real.

Glimpsing the glory of God and sensing His nearness are the essentials. Messages that shake, comfort, or teach us come through on these tracks of spiritual communication. Maybe it's like this: Three children in a grade school science class were given an assignment. "At home tonight, count the stars when they come out. Do it right in your own yard." Next day they reported. "I counted 128!" exclaimed one girl. Another saw 78. A small boy could report seeing only 23. "Why so few when all the stars were out last night and the others saw so many?" "Well, we have a very small yard," explained the lad.

Look and listen now to a breathtaking picture of what worship was. It can be seen clearly, even from the small yards of small churches. The scene is a moment of worship, coming from long ago (2 Chron. 5:11-14 NIV).

All the priests who were there had consecrated themselves, regardless of their divisions. All the Levites who were musicians...and their sons and relatives—stood on the east side of the altar, dressed in fine linen and playing cymbals, harps and lyres. They were accompanied by 120 priests sounding trumpets. The trumpeters and singers joined in unison, as with one voice, to give praise and thanks to the Lord...and sang: "He is good; His love endures forever."

Then the temple of the Lord was filled with a cloud, and the priests could not perform their service because of the cloud, for the glory of the Lord filled the temple of God.

Imagine glory, like a cloud, so thick the musicians couldn't even see to read their notes! This must have meant that 120 trumpeters, the cymbalists, harpists, and singers stopped dead still in silent worship. The glory of the Lord filled the place. It was overpowering. Like Elijah learned watching "a great and powerful wind [that] tore the mountains apart and shattered the rocks before the Lord....After the wind there was an earthquake....After the earthquake came a fire...." But the Lord was not in the wind...the Lord was not in the earthquake...the Lord was not in the fire. "And after the fire came a gentle whisper." (1 Kings 19:11, 12 NIV) Elijah heard it, and Elijah listened.

How much does it take for God to get our attention? All the great and beautiful things that happen in worship are simply to glorify God and prepare us to listen to Him. But a Solomon-sized cathedral is not necessary for this sort of worship. The point is, *God is still speaking*. This we believe, really believe, but one doesn't always hear. Watching worshipers coming and going makes one wonder also if others do. Unless we see the wonder and listen to the "gentle whispers," church and all it is supposed to be becomes insipid, boring, and/or just another entertainment requiring good performers. This easily moves into competition for the better platform actors. The core question is not "Are my needs being met?" or, "Is church fun?" but "Have we listened and heard from God?" Is Truth grasped and are we convicted of wrongdoing and motivated to obedience?

Here is another scene. Worship is not always even pleasant to be real. This total contrast to the noise and silence just described is a close-up look at one person (maybe surrounded by a few gawking critics). It is Job, Old Testament Job. The most despicable, hopeless, uninviting spectacle one can imagine. Job, gasping, at the terrible end of his very worst experience; Job, who has hung in there so far, who has "not cursed God" nor denied his faith in a redeeming Creator; Job, now reeling, staggering, stinking, and…lonely, has just dispatched his three friends. Eliphaz, Bildad, and Zophar have finally run out of advice.

Don't switch channels yet, or pronounce the benediction. We must sit in with one who is nursing boils, in financial bankruptcy, a broken man, mourning the loss of loved ones and all his possessions. He is in worship! And God is speaking. It is one of the longest, most detailed speeches directly from God recorded. Now we know it all turned out okay, but Job didn't see it yet. This poor, innocent brother wiped out with tragedies shows why worship is not just the last resort, it is the only one sometimes.

One might suppose God would be saying something comforting. God has to, to fit our stereotype of a fair, forgiving, prayer-answering deity. It is seen, however, that a visitation and the messages of the Spirit cannot be scheduled, monitored, or controlled. God is in charge of worship, or we are, and it is often more manageable if we are.

God ought to be saying, "Job, bless your heart, you've had a very bad time and I am sorry. Now come on out of that awful pile of ashes. Get a hot shower. I have some good news for you. You're going to become famous forever. There will even be a lovely organization called Job's Daughters...."

God didn't. What did God say? Let's listen in (from Job, chapters 37 and 38 NIV):

"Listen to this, Job; stop and consider God's wonders. Do you know how God controls the clouds and makes his lightning flash? Do you know how the clouds hang poised, those wonders of him who is perfect in knowledge? You who swelter in your clothes when the land lies hushed under the south wind, can you join him in spreading out the skies, hard as a mirror of cast bronze?

"Tell us what we should say to him....no one can look at the sun, bright as it is in the skies after the wind has swept them clean. Out of the north he comes in golden splendor; God comes in awesome majesty. The Almighty is beyond our reach and exalted in power; in his justice and great righteousness, he does not oppress. Therefore, men revere him, for does he not have regard for all the wise in heart?"

The service goes on.

"Where were you when I laid the earth's foundation? Tell me, if you understand. Who marked off its dimensions? Surely you know! Who stretched a measuring line across it? On what were its footings set, or who laid its cornerstone—while the morning stars sang together and all the angels shouted for joy?

*   *   *   *   *

"Have you ever given orders to the morning, or shown the dawn its place, that it might take the earth by the edges and shake the wicked out of it? The earth takes shape like clay under a seal; its features stand out like those of a garment....

"Have you journeyed to the springs of the sea or walked in the recesses of the deep? Have the gates of death been shown to you? Have you seen the gates of the shadow of death? Have you comprehended the vast expanses of the earth? Tell me if you know all this."

This gives us clues about the meaning and practice of worship. It is useful for those of us who are impatient or complacent, who insist on neat, fine-tuned, total worship. When God really gets through to us, it makes a difference.

Did you know God talks to Job about His creativity in making all sorts of things, such as whales, ostriches, coyotes, and spiders, not to mention the weather, mountains, oceans, and the universe? In essence He says, "Job, you see all these things; do you find any fault?"

Confronted with this massive exhibit of God's greatness, Job was humbled and reassured. Worship is also confrontation. No wonder Job put his hand over his mouth murmuring, "I've said too much already." Haven't we all been in worship wishing the same thing for ourselves—and for a few others?

Worship is being with God. How does one behave, act, or think in His Presence? "Don't touch the Ark of the Covenant!" the ancient Jews were warned. It represented the Presence. "Stay out of the 'Holy of Holies'"...until the curtain was opened from top to bottom. Being in worship, with God there, is one of life's most momentous experiences. How can we miss it? There is nothing at all casual about worship. Watching space shuttle views and telestar photos, storms and sunrises are impressive, but having the Spirit pinpoint our personal situation with His Light and Love brings a whole new view of ourselves and the world. The worship act is like the shocks of birth and death; one's inner being is convulsed or shaken. All these fundamental things of life surface in worship, enabling a person and God together a breakthrough that transcends the work-a-day world, and the tragic ordinariness of so many church services that are called worship.

Some seem to have the notion that worship at its best requires a lot of emotional response. Or that really good worshipers (and worship services) appeal mostly to philosophers and poets or those with arty tastes, those who "wonder with marveling and with that which makes us marvel." (Josef Pieper) Yet, history is filled with coolheaded, sensible people, not greatly moved by the romantic blurring around them, who worshiped and walked with God. There is needed now more hardheaded and softhearted, sensible Christians not carried along with religious fads or politicized and culturized Christianity. Remember, worship is primarily an inward, and at the same time, a very reasonable experience. God is neither foolish nor fanatical.

Worship is a discipline. It is spiritual work. Perhaps this sign should hang in the church foyer: "Worship is not restful relaxing. It is work!" It is to be learned, like tennis or piano playing or any other discipline. Not a stressful, exhausting thing, but it is work in the sense of concentration for listening. Real hearing takes at least three things: concentration, remembering, and application.

The consequence of worship is that we are changed, according to Richard Foster. So, if worship does not change us, it has not been worship at all. To stand before the Holy One of eternity, who knows us yet loves us, is transforming. Resentments, for instance, or self-pity or despair, cannot be held with the same tenacity when we enter His gracious light. Jesus said that we are to leave our gift at the altar and go set the matter straight (Matt. 5:23, 24). If worship "does not propel us into greater obedience," it has not been worship, Foster insists in his writing on the subject.

An illustration has been helpful to me. There are different ways of looking at a rose. One can simply be pleasantly aware of it, or *look* at it, seeing its color, kind, and size. This may bring great enjoyment. But to really *observe* (study) it, is something else. One begins to count the petals, or take measurements, or make comparisons. This sort of observation is a demanding activity, what a botanist calls "an act of aggression." This is different from mere contemplation, to enjoy its beauty for a moment.

What about spiritual contemplation and studied listening? It is possible to participate in worship with an awareness that something pleasant is happening. Then there is the "aggressive act" of an attitude of complete receptivity, openness to the Spirit, taking measurements of our lives. We believe in the reality of finding and knowing God, and here part company with those who just "go to church" as a commendable habit. Church services can be quite meaningless, or religious games skillfully played, even with great energy and enjoyment.

Many of the Old Testament teachings about worship and preparation for it, along with the last words of Jesus before His ascension, take us into the studied experience of waiting (in prayer and obedience) until the Comforter comes to bring power as witnesses. All this emphasized the work and wonder of worship.

This brings us to the realization that unpredictable spontaneity in worship is a myth, albeit an appealing one. Younger Christians and sometimes pastors assume that if we could dismantle all tradition, order, structures, and conventions we would just be free, direct, and *spontaneous*. If this is what some have in mind for "open worship" as announced in the church bulletin, the point and purpose are missed. Open worship can be a dangerous disgrace unless the time and exercise is used by carefully prepared hearts in participation. It is not a synonym for impulsiveness or empty-headedness, or off-the-cuff religious prattle. Nor is it the chance to tell about Uncle John's arthritic-problem-for-prayer today. Uncle John may need prayer, as do his concerned relatives reporting it, but like Job and his boils, we need first to see the heavens before pointing out problems on the horizon. There are times and settings entirely appropriate for this kind of prayer and loving concern, but morning worship belongs to God and us together.

Here is another borrowed illustration: "What if you paid twenty dollars to hear a performance of Beethoven's *Seventh Symphony* and the orchestra straggled into the hall late. The director rushes in breathlessly announcing: 'Wow! Have we had a busy week. Lots of travel, recording sessions, now here we are and we haven't had a chance to rehearse for this concert. Listen, I have a great idea. Everyone here likes music, so what do you say we just have a jam session, let it flow. Be spontaneous!'" (Ben Patterson in *Leadership* magazine)

What does this mean pragmatically? It means something like a good night's sleep on Saturday night and getting up in time to prepare unhurriedly for meeting with God and other disciples at worship. Habitual Sunday morning tardiness and tiredness is a theological issue.

It means giving as much attention to preparing our attitude for worship as we do our appearance. It means "prayed-upness" on the part of the pastor with conscientious preparation of the message, as well as the bulletin, the selection of songs, the appearance of the room and the grounds, and even the appearance of the people and the preacher. These all relate to the theology and experience of worship! Upholstered pews and stained glass windows are not nearly as important (although they can be helpful) as seeing to it that dust, cobwebs, last week's Sunday school papers, and out-dated stuff on bulletin boards—all these things—are cared for properly. Squeaky clean vestibules and sanctuaries are next to godliness.

An anything-is-all-right-since-it's-only-church attitude is an affront to the Guest Presence in the Midst. It seems that some actually take pride in cluttered churches as though that is a sign of humility or modesty. It is sloppy stewardship. It implies to ourselves and any visitors that worship isn't really very important. Boring buildings contribute to boring services. This is not a call for ostentation, expensive furnishing or architecture, rather, a plea for being sure that what we have is clean, ready, and as comfortable as possible.

Related to this is how to evaluate variety in the worship experiences. It is okay to "use" variety since it is people who worship and God made all kinds. Perhaps it is proper to start worship with snappy choruses or with silent prayer once in a while. But only when it is "edifying" to the Body and not some whim or tangent of a leader.

About silent prayer: When the meeting worships in silence it should be silent, not interrupted with soft music. Background music in total silence is not silent, it is very noticeable. There is a time for both, but not together!

By variety is meant such things as changing the order of service, or introducing innovative content. When this is done, even in planning for it (very carefully), it is terribly important to make things very clear. When there are changes, especially dramatic ones, careful and repeated explanation, preparation, and guidance is necessary. Nothing is more upsetting than worship interrupted with strange kinds of goings on that are not anticipated. Nevertheless even dramatic innovations can be meaningful if handled carefully and prayerfully.

Public prayers, as well as pastoral prayers, are to be representational. They are never to be used for display of praying skills, or for making subtle announcements, or the repreaching of the sermon. Nor for scolding. In 2 Chronicles, chapter six, is found Solomon's public prayer, where he referred 94 times to God, but 81 times to the people. That is probably a proper ratio.

Are you going to read the Scripture, or anything else, aloud? Practice. Rehearse, rehearse, rehearse. The same goes for preaching as well as singing.

In worship, why is a special song "special"? Special words, special music, or special singer? Maybe others understand, but the more special billing a performance gets in worship, the less spiritual it seems. Also, it is reported that in many churches 20 hymns out of 500 possible selections are used. There is a place for rich variety.

One more word about public announcements. There is an art in getting all the facts and emphasis possible in a brief and an appropriate time. Bear in mind that most churchgoers are believed to be literate, that is, able to read printed-in-the-bulletin material. Creative ways can be used to encourage promotion of events and news that avoid excessive time interrupting worship. Public pleading for volunteers for any program before a captive worship gathering is disgraceful, and more effectively done in other ways.

Psalm 34 has been cited by Ann Ortlund (*Up With Worship,* Word, 1978) as a worship model. David, she insists, did not whip it out on the spur of the moment. The whole psalm is an acrostic. This means that the Hebrew alphabet is built into the first letter of each line, beautifully. That takes effort to make it come out right.

I will extol the Lord at all times, his praise will always
   be on my lips.
My soul will boast in the Lord; let the afflicted hear
   and rejoice.
Glorify the Lord with me; let us exalt his name
   together.

I sought the Lord, and he answered me; he delivered
   me from all my fears.
Those who look to him are radiant; their faces are
   never covered with shame.
This poor man called, and the Lord heard him; he
   saved him out of all his troubles.
The angel of the Lord encamps around those who fear
   him, and he delivers them.

Taste and see that the Lord is good; blessed is the man
   who takes refuge in him.
Fear the Lord, you his saints, for those who fear him
   lack nothing....

The eyes of the Lord are on the righteous and his ears
   are attentive to their cry; the face of the Lord is
   against those who do evil, to cut off the memory of
   them from the earth.

The righteous cry out, and the Lord hears them; he
   delivers them from all their troubles.
The Lord is close to the brokenhearted and saves
   those who are crushed in spirit.   *—NIV*

That is worship. Anything that is not God-directed is but a faint echo of praise to Him, the real purpose of real worship.

Aimless worship is sharpened and focused by remembering that it is not worship we worship, nor the form, nor (heaven help us) the pastor. It is God we worship! Our worship has only one Leader, Jesus our Lord. It is He who is present. It is His voice heard in our hearts, His nearness that is sensed. We, by faith, find we not only read about Him in Scripture, we can know Him by revelation. He is there. This Truth, even when only partly grasped, can be seen to have a certain dignity, a majesty. This is testimony. We sense that we have an obligation and opportunity to listen, to watch, to respond.

Worship is built into our own makeup. We are created for worship just as God is always seeking worshipers. The search for fresh reassurance of the reality of our relationship with God and fellow disciples is entirely appropriate. It means we are alive. We all need guidance and direction, healing, and help. "God is made perfect in our weakness."

This is not to say that worship is easy or natural, even though it is built into our nature. Those who decide not to worship don't succeed in not worshiping, they just turn to some form of idolatry. When Jesus said, "True worshipers will worship the Father in spirit and truth" (John 4:23 NIV), He was simply assuming people will worship. They always do. The important thing is to do it in spirit and in truth. When one worships a mountain, or some guru, he will receive what a mountain or a guru has to offer.

Worship, it has been said, allows our uniqueness as a people and as a church to belong to God who gave it. To simply be shaped into some kind of religious or denominational mold is to miss the point. This is as unfortunate as attempting to stamp everyone into the same personality mold. Church, our church, is to allow everyone to serve the Lord in the beauty of holiness and in their own uniqueness. "The truth shall make you free...." It is the inhibitions, fear, selfishness, ignorance of our own identity as Friends and the convictions bonding us together, the bound-up or competitive feelings—these are the things that prevent freedom in worship.

To be one in the Spirit is true togetherness. Not that we look alike, dress alike, sound alike, or even think alike. We are one in the Spirit because in Christ we dare to be ourselves. "Take my yoke upon you," Jesus said. We are not to be yokeless, but hear Him saying, "learn of me, for my yoke is easy and my burden is light." (Matt. 11:30 KJV)

Worship is a deliberate and disciplined adventure in reality. It is not for the irreverent or comfortable. It involves an opening of ourselves to the delightful and at the same time dangerous life of the Spirit. It makes all the religious paraphernalia of temples and priests, rites and ceremonies irrelevant. It involves a willingness to "Let the word of Christ dwell in you richly, teach and admonish one another in all wisdom, and sing psalms and spiritual songs with thankfulness in your hearts to God." (Col. 3:16 RSV)[1]

1. Adapted from Willard Sperry, "Reality in Worship" taken from *Celebration of Discipline*, Richard Foster, p. 149.

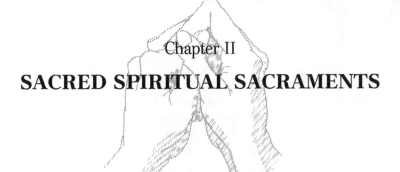

Chapter II

SACRED SPIRITUAL SACRAMENTS

Wait for the gift my Father promised...for John baptized
with water, but...you will be baptized with the Holy
Spirit....You will receive power when the Holy Spirit
comes on you; and you will be my witnesses....
—Acts 1:4-8 NIV

Jesus said to them, "I tell you the truth, unless you eat the flesh of the
Son of Man and drink his blood, you have no life in you....Just as the
living Father sent me and I live because of the Father, so the one who
feeds on me will live because of me."—John 6:53, 57 NIV

What do Friends believe about baptism and communion? Those acquainted with Quakers learn we don't practice the "out-ward ordinances," but too often it is never understood why. Unfortunately, many Friends themselves don't understand why either!

It is the superficial understanding of a very important teaching of the Gospel and the faith and practice of the church that must be considered. Our loyalties to the church, as well as any disagreements, if they exist, should be based on accurate understanding of the Scriptures, the nature of the church, and sound doctrine. "Truth," someone has said, "must become our own truth, or it is not real to us." It is as important to know precisely *what* we believe as what we may not believe.

19

Discovering that a Quaker experience of baptism and communion are crucial to our faith is as important as breathing. The infilling of the Holy Spirit through the grace and power of God is a vital part of day-to-day living; this fact makes this entire subject one of special significance.

The reflections to follow on this are reverently shared in humility. This is not a debate, not an argument. It is a testimony. Like the most precious and intimate experiences with one's own family and loved ones, the emotional feelings deep within confirm the depth of this precious practice and teaching.

In reviewing the Scriptures we will be examining, one wants to kneel in gratitude and worship. Sacraments are sacred, they are part of the divine plan of salvation through the blood of Christ shed on Calvary. They are considered in a spirit of tenderness, of reverent adoration of God.

Not only is this matter discussed positively and not negatively, it is also an issue raised without apology. When as Christians our faith rests firmly on the Scriptures resulting from Christ's revealing and redeeming work, we can freely and openly express our convictions, not defensively, but exuberantly. It has also been possible to test the validity of these truths, the teachings of Jesus concerning the sacraments, not only from personal experience but as a missionary and pastor for many years, from observing His work and power in the lives of others.

Truth is not arrived at by majority vote. Neither does one wisely take a position merely to be different, nor to sit in judgment on the wider Christian fellowship in worship practice or Christian living. Because Friends believe as deeply as we do, it would be dishonest or misleading to miss an opportunity to bear witness to those who may not understand as we do the Bible teachings on the meaning of the sacraments. There is found, especially in this generation, a genuine search for deeper truth and basic beliefs. It is superficiality, the following of religious celebrities, popular or traditional "churchianity," or the blind following of denominationalism as an end in itself that is being rejected by thoughtful younger and newer Christians.

This is good. It provides a place and opportunity for positive, radiant witness of our faith. Why, then, do Friends sometimes assume an apologetic or negative stance with fleeting or inadequate references such as, "Quakers do not practice the ordinances," or, "Friends don't baptize or take communion." One must immediately exclaim, "But Quakers *do* practice the worship and discipleship procedures taught in the Bible. We do believe in baptism. We live in and on our communion with the Lord and with one another in the faith." Without these sacred and beautiful experiences our lives are empty and powerless. Daily partaking of the "Bread of Life" provides the energy for witness to those about us.

The "outward evidence" of God's grace in our lives is carefully explained by our Lord: "All men will know that you are my disciples if you love one another." (John 13:35 NIV) This is the distinguishing characteristic for Christians, not a symbol, not a sign, not one public act. It is a way of life, a way of living made possible only by the power of God, the inner cleansing, abiding presence and daily submission of ourselves to the Holy Spirit. "John baptized with water," Jesus said just before His ascension, "but...you will be baptized with the Holy Spirit." (Acts 1:5 NIV) And, they were and we are too if we "wait for the gift my Father promised." (Acts 1:4 NIV)

Apparently this is what Paul had in mind in writing to the Ephesian Christians when speaking of "one body and one Spirit...one hope...one Lord, one faith, one baptism; one God and Father of all, who is over all and through all and in all." (Eph. 4:4-6 NIV) "One" baptism? Happily it is Jesus' baptism with the Holy Spirit as He promised, rather than John's, which was finished.

Apparently it is what our Lord had in mind when giving the missionary commandment: "Therefore go and make dis-

ciples of all nations, baptizing them in *the name* of the Father
and of the Son and of the Holy Spirit." (Matt. 28:19 NIV) Then
Jesus adds the specific result of this, repeating what He had
earlier urged, "This is my command, that you love each other.
All men will know that you are my disciples if you love one
another." So, the completed commission of the Great
Commission is "…teaching them [new disciples] to obey everything I have commanded you." (Matt. 28:20 NIV)

A baptismal initiation, by definition, is just that—a new
beginning. To be "washed…sanctified…justified in the name
of the Lord Jesus Christ and *by the Spirit* of our God" (1 Cor.
6:11 NIV) is certainly a marvelous initiation! Paul reminded
Titus of the same fact of faith, saying, "He saved us through
the washing of rebirth and renewal *by the Holy Spirit*, whom he
poured out on us generously through Jesus Christ our Savior."
(Titus 3:5, 6 NIV)

A singularly clear and helpful explanation comes from
Hebrews 8:10. Reviewing several features of the Jewish tabernacle worship, the function of priests, the "Holy Place," it
concludes saying, "This is an illustration…indicating that the
gifts and sacrifices being offered were not able to clear the
conscience of the worshiper. They are only a matter of food
and drink and various ceremonial washings—external regulations applying until the time of the new order." (Heb. 9:9, 10
NIV)

The new order? The church. It began on Pentecost Day
when Jesus' promise of the baptism of the Holy Spirit really
happened. We are yet enjoying the new order, until the next,
when Jesus comes again for another new order—a new heav-
en, a new earth with all of us in new bodies "like unto his!"

God seems to have chosen the use of signs, symbols, badges as
being important to identify His chosen people. For instance,
when God appeared to Abram in Ur of the Chaldees He told
Abram that he was to leave his former life and his home ties.

By faith, Abram did it. He began a complete move, heading out for the "promised land." But God did a curious thing then. He insisted on sealing the call with a sign, one that lasts to this day among the "children of Abraham." "Then God said to Abraham, 'as for you, you must keep my covenant, you and your descendants after you for the generations to come. This is my covenant...every male among you shall be circumcised...it will be the sign of the covenant between you and me.'" (Gen. 17:9-11 NIV) This sign continued as a special relationship covenant between this chosen man and his God.

Another badge given much later occurred with the children of Abraham, numbering at the time in the hundreds of thousands. They were being delivered out of slavery in Egypt under Moses' leadership. The circumcision sign was, of course, still used. Now, here came another: "Remember the sabbath day, to keep it holy. Six days shalt thou labor, and do all thy work: but the seventh day is a sabbath of the Lord thy God." (Exodus 20:8-10 KJV)

It was hammered into their culture again and again. "The Lord spoke to Moses, saying, speak also unto the children of Israel, saying, verily my sabbaths you shall keep: for *it is a sign* between me and you throughout your generations." God was specific, even more so than about circumcision. Exodus chapter 31 gives the details.

It is not until the ministry of John the Baptist that there is mention of another identifying sign in the nation of Israel. John's ministry was new and unique. He preached to people who professed to believe the promises of the Old Testament. Many accepted him as another prophet sent from God. His audiences by and large were Jewish, and they, of course, were all sabbath-observing people—circumcision was practiced religiously—and now a third identifying sign was stated, the sign of water baptism in the Jordan River. This act indicated they believed God was about to send the Messiah, the Redeemer they had been waiting for, and they prepared to receive Him in repentance of their sins. This was a sign of preparation and expectancy.

Here is another scene. It has been painted and reprinted perhaps more than any other New Testament account. It is the "Last Supper," Jesus with the twelve disciples observing the Passover feast around a table. The Gospel of John, chapter 13, describes it. Before quoting word for word, it should be mentioned that Judas has just left the room. Because of this, it was a tense moment. The other disciples, trying to absorb the implications of the drama unfolding, heard Jesus saying:

> My children, I will be with you only a little longer. You will look for me, and just as I told the Jews, so I tell you now: Where I am going, you cannot come.

> A new commandment I give you: Love one another. As I have loved you, so you must love one another. All men will know that you are my disciples if you love one another.   —*NIV*

Isn't this what Christians are supposed to do "in remembrance" of Him?

This sign, of Christian love, is the "mark of the Christian." (Francis Schaeffer) Abram's covenant sign of circumcision meant his old life was changed, his former culture was replaced with another. Moses' instruction to command the keeping of the sabbath was a sign of obedience and respect for God. Both are kept to this day by the Jewish people. John the Baptist, who reluctantly baptized Jesus in the Jordan River since Jesus did not need to repent, was instructed that he, John, would "decrease," while Christ would "increase." "The man on whom you see the Spirit come down and remain is he who will baptize with the Holy Spirit." (John 1:33 NIV) As far as we know Jesus never baptized anyone with water.

The love of believers for fellow Christians was and is a new identifying mark of true discipleship. It was said of the Christians after their baptism by Christ on Pentecost Day with the Holy Spirit: "Behold how they love one another!" That is a good sign. Just as a child of Abraham would never be recognized as a true Israelite if uncircumcised, and any Israelite who failed to keep the sabbath would be cut off, or one could not be counted a disciple of John without water baptism, our Lord said *His* disciples will be identified with this sign: "Love one another."

This must be carried further. All the ordinances of the Old Testament and those developed by various churches and denominations (these vary according to the practice and preference of each) can be administered by a person, or prepared by people. Only Christ can produce love within our hearts; this is possible only by the power of the Holy Spirit. No one can be browbeaten or scolded or even led into loving; only God, by pouring His Spirit into our hearts, by cleansing our inner lives, can enable us to show the genuine sign of the mark of a Christian—love.

Do you see why it is so crucial that we understand the meaning of baptism—true baptism, the baptism John saw in saying, "I indeed baptize with water, but you shall be baptized with the Holy Spirit"?

Christ was circumcised, kept the sabbath, was baptized of John, and died on the cross, but His disciples were *not to follow Him in any* of these any longer. They were instead to be what Jesus was—Love. "As the Father hath loved me, so have I loved you: *continue...*in my love." (John 15:9 KJV)

Paul beautifully expressed this priority in the "Love Chapter." Of all the graces and qualities of "faith, hope and love...the greatest of these is love." (1 Cor. 13:13 NIV)

This brings us to the Scripture Friends use often and from which we get the name "Friends." "This is my commandment, That ye love one another, as I have loved you. Greater love hath no man than this, that a man lay down his life for his friends. Ye are my friends if ye do whatsoever I command you." (John 15:12-14 KJV) Love of this depth is the outward sign of an inward work of grace. It expresses itself in our understanding of peacemaking; it expresses itself in our gospel witness as missionaries, in evangelism, in social concerns, and in all aspects of faith and practice.

It is emphasized urgently in Paul's writing: "I beg you...to live and act in a way worthy of those who have been chosen for such wonderful blessings." He spells it out to the Ephesian Christians, and to us. "Be humble and gentle. Be patient with each other, and make allowances for each other's faults because of your love....We are all parts of one body, we have the same Spirit, and we have all been called to the same glorious future." (Eph. 4:1-4 TLB) This is keeping the ordinances, the New Testament worship practices in human relationships and behavior. Love is the more excellent way.

Why then is it so crucially important, even urgent, that those who are Friends by convincement and understanding of God's revealed truth in Scripture be completely clear in their understanding of a proper "keeping of the ordinances"? Eventually every person is responsible to God for his acceptance or rejection of the Gospel. Each individual believer builds the Christian life on his or her own personal relationship with God. ("...work out your salvation with fear and trembling, for it is God who works in you to will and to act according to his good purpose." Phil. 2:12, 13 NIV) But God also deals with each one through the Body, the Church, and on biblical grounds; the role of the Body and one's denominational connection is neglected only at great peril to our spiritual growth and effectiveness. When we are thoughtfully and honestly searching, we can discover the essential values that lie beneath many of the positions held. Indeed we *must* discover them to have a substantial faith. We therefore need to learn what basic truth is and incorporate it into our own faith and practice as maturing followers of Christ. To neglect to do this leaves us shallow in faith, subject to only cultural Christianity, or worse, vulnerable to any cult or popular practice of religion presented as being a church.

When Paul wrote to the Galatians, saying, "In Jesus Christ neither circumcision availeth any thing, nor uncircumcision; but faith which worketh by love" (Gal. 5:6 KJV), he set forth the correct attitude, not of a denomination, but of the entire Christian church, toward all outward ordinances. A denomination is meaningless if it reaches the place where it expresses no testimony concerning the things that make it different from other denominations. This pinpoints the importance of a specific denominational connection. Our distinctive faith rests on a careful interpretation of Scripture and the concepts behind it. Here are discovered certain doctrinal landmarks that make Friends a distinct and vital group.

Probably some who have read this far will become impatient with additional examination, being either already convinced and ready to leave the subject or hurry on to something else. Others may fear upsetting previously held practices or persuasion or find it easier to simply avoid further exploration of the subject.

However, given the significance of the truth under consideration, patient, careful, detailed study is called for. It may be like a navigator on a plane checking his course, it has to be right! Or like a surgeon preparing for surgery, a casual or disinterested approach to the task is unthinkable. So with our approach to the subjects of baptism and communion.

It is important to take a long look at the meaning of covenants. There are the old covenants of the Old Testament, and new covenants in the New Testament. Paul drew the contrast well: Christ has enabled us to be "ministers of a new covenant—not of the letter but of the Spirit; for the letter kills but the Spirit gives life." (2 Cor. 3:6 NIV) The Old Testament worship practice in tabernacles, temples, ceremonies, and priestly functions was absolutely according to the letter of the Law. They killed a lamb, they put blood on the doorposts, they kept the Passover in exactly the right way and time. Only the

priests and the High Priests could lead in many of the ceremonial rites. "The first covenant had regulations for worship
and also an earthly sanctuary." (Heb. 9:1 NIV) There follows
in that passage a description of all the paraphernalia in this
tabernacle. The priest officiated, using the furniture in a specific way. The church, of the new covenant, has a greater High
Priest who officiates (Heb. 8:2 NIV) "in the sanctuary, the true
tabernacle set up by the Lord, not by man."

We see that the nature of the church is a spiritual organ-
ism, composed of spiritual people, who become such by being
filled with the Holy Spirit. Since "that which is born of the flesh
is flesh; and that which is born of the Spirit is spirit" (John 3:6
KJV), it is impossible that as spiritual people we should either
be produced or nourished by material things. It is not a phys-
ical act anymore; the new covenant is a spiritual relationship
of the "inner being." References to water and fire, the door, the
way, the light are no longer literal but figurative. The spiritual
life for the Christian in the church is not to be sustained with
literal tabernacle ceremonies as in the past, but sustained and
nourished only as we "eat the flesh of the Son of Man and
drink his blood" in the sense that Jesus meant it (John 6:53, 63
NIV). "The Spirit gives life; the flesh counts for nothing. The
words I have spoken to you are spirit and they are life." (It
merits mentioning that it was following this saying of Jesus that
it is reported in verse 66, "From this time many of his disciples
turned back and no longer followed him.")

To attach spiritual value to an outward ordinance is to
make it a substitute for the Spirit's work in our lives, and thus
easily leads to a form of idolatry in which these things and
practices receive the honor and importance due only to God.
The hour "now is, when the true worshippers shall worship the
Father in spirit and in truth: for the Father seeketh such to
worship him." (John 4:23 KJV)

The Christian, you see, is removed from the ceremonial
performances of the past when he comes to realize his position in Christ. As long as one depends on ceremony, or some

particular manner of performing that ceremony, many questions and dangers are raised.

For instance, regarding the ordinance of water baptism, the question arises what persons (priest or pastor or who) is eligible to do it? When should it be done? How...immersion, sprinkling, for infants, for joining a church? These are serious questions puzzling many. A reassuring answer is found in Colossians 2:10-12 KJV: "Ye are complete in him, which is the head of all principality and power: in whom also you are circumcised with the circumcision made without hands, in putting off the body of the sins of the flesh by the circumcision of Christ: buried with him in baptism, wherein also you are risen with him through the faith of the operation of God, who hath raised him from the dead."

Our natural birth into the human family brings upon us the penalty of the sin of Adam. In like manner our spiritual birth, which is entirely by faith, puts us "in Christ," so that everything that He did that was righteous or ceremonial is credited to us.

In the verse just mentioned from Colossians, only baptism and circumcision are mentioned. Jesus fulfilled both as well as all others, of course. The circumcision of Christ, which was done on the eighth day (Luke 2:21), fulfills that obligation for everyone that is *in Christ*. The baptism of Jesus by John in the river Jordan fulfills for every member of the church, who is in Him, the obligation of having that ceremony performed. Jesus, of His own account, needed neither. But as our substitute, He went through these ceremonies that we might be released from them and know the reality behind each act.

Instead of Christians having to be baptized because Christ was baptized, the fact that He was baptized is the very reason we do not need to be! In fact, once we grasp the scope of all that Jesus did for us in exclaiming on the cross, "It is finished!" it seems a mockery for us to try to do something in the flesh to add to what He has done at such cost. To do so is really questioning whether all He has done is really sufficient.

What is to be done with the statement of Jesus found in Mark 16:16 (KJV): "He that believeth and is baptized shall be saved; but he that believeth not shall be damned"? Remember the two baptisms: John's and Jesus'? Since water is not here mentioned, Jesus is evidently speaking of His own rather than John's baptism. It is important to notice the tense of the verb "is" rather than "has been." If this is intended to be water baptism and immersion the method, it would mean keeping under water a very long time! The baptism of Jesus is a process, not an act; it is an abiding baptism, working a continuing as well as permanent change.

There comes to mind, of course, the various references indicating the practice of water baptism in different forms and times in the early church as described in the Book of Acts and elsewhere. In the 14 epistles of Paul, including the one to the Hebrews, the word "baptism" is found three times, "baptize" once, "baptized" 12 times, and "baptisms" once. This means 17 times in Paul's writing, and once in Peter's epistle.

There are some observations on this that may be helpful. If in the 21 epistles, 14 are entirely silent on the subject, we could assume that baptism is not of first importance in their teaching. If, however, these few references show that water baptism is essential to salvation, or even necessary in order to be fully obedient to the Lord, we must take a serious look at the matter. One thing is that the word *water* is not used in connection with the mention of baptism in any of these passages. That in itself is significant. Examination of the passages one by one reveals the following: The six times the words occur in 1 Corinthians 1:13-17 the inference is quite plain that Paul is talking about water baptism but as an explanation of his usage of the ordinance rather than a vindication or defining it as a requirement. He thanks God he did not baptize any more than he did, and concludes the whole subject by saying that God did not send him to baptize but to preach the Gospel. This could indicate he thought that water baptism had no part of the Gospel of Christ.

It has already been mentioned that in Ephesians 4:5 (KJV) it is clear one could reasonably conclude the "one Lord, one faith, one baptism..." refers to Jesus' rather than John's baptism.

Peter's one reference to the subject in 1 Peter 3:21 (KJV) draws attention back to the flood, "the like figure whereunto even baptism doth also now save us." Reading the surrounding context of this, one discovers Peter guards against interpretation of water being a regeneration element by saying in the same verse, "not the putting away of the filth of the flesh," which would result from washing with water, "but the answer of a good conscience toward God, by the resurrection of Jesus Christ."

It is interesting to read again the story of Peter's visit to the house of Cornelius. After repeated visions of some kind of a sheet being lowered from heaven with all sorts of forbidden food for a Jew to eat, Peter is told to eat anyway. This prepared him for his visit and meal with Cornelius (Acts 10). After the whole episode, Peter was reporting it all to others back in Jerusalem, pointing out how remarkable it was that the Holy Spirit came on them even in the house of a Gentile! At this point Peter suddenly added, "Then I remembered what the Lord had said, 'John baptized with water, but you will be baptized with the Holy Spirit.'" (Acts 11:16 NIV) It appears Peter all at once put together in his comprehension the whole transition from the Old Testament Jewish practices to the new era of the church. It is worth noting that after Acts 11, there is no reference to Peter's use or encouragement of water baptism.

This leads to an evaluation of the amount of material and emphasis given in the Book of Acts regarding water baptism and communion. In the Old Testament, when an ordinance was instituted, there were given specific instructions as to how to do it and when. Take, for example, the Passover lamb. They were told precisely the kind of lamb it was to be, when it was to be selected, just when it was to be killed, and the very places the blood was to be put, the kind of herb with which the blood was to be conveyed to the doorposts, and so on. Five different kinds of sacrifices in Leviticus, chapters one through seven, are detailed. If outward ordinances of the church were to be as explicit and ongoing as these, surely there would be more time and specificity to the matter in the New Testament writings.

We know, of course, that the apostles and other early Christians at times baptized new converts in water. We know too that the Book of Acts is a history of the transition period between the two dispensations of Law and Grace. The veil of the Temple was rent asunder the day Jesus died, and, so far as practical value is concerned, the Old Testament ceremonial system lost its power that day. The Book of Acts covers a greater part of half a century, a time when emotional as well as theological difficulties were involved in making this transition. For at least a part of this period, the apostles apparently also continued Jewish feasts and temple ordinances. Circumcision was practiced. The whole argument of circumcision became a major discussion in the Jerusalem Council (Acts 15, 16).

Why did Jesus not give more instructions regarding these things to the disciples or instruct them not to continue in them? In John 16:12, 13 (KJV), He explained: "I have yet many things to say unto you, but you cannot bear them now. However, when he the Spirit of truth is come, he will guide you into all truth: for he shall not speak of himself; but whatsoever he shall hear, that shall he speak: and he will show you things to come. He shall glorify me; for He shall receive of mine, and shall show it unto you." Much of the Book of Acts is an account of the process by which the Holy Spirit led the apostles in the early church in the formulation of governing and practices of the new church. While we know that one is regenerated through forgiveness of sins and accepts Christ as Savior in an instant of time, and also that one receives the infilling of the Holy Spirit by faith, we know that neither of these acts removes instantly residual prejudices nor instantaneously brings correct form of religious practices. Maturity comes step by step in adding knowledge to faith.

The Galatian epistle indicates that there was a determined effort on the part of some of the Jews who had become Christians to load the church with all the Old Testament ordinances, and Paul had some of his most persistent struggles with people who tried to retain these in the church.

Another comment on the subject of baptism is taken from the *Constitution and Discipline* of Northwest Yearly Meeting of Friends Church (1979, p. 21). "We would express our continued conviction that our Lord appointed no outward rite or ceremony for observance in His church. We accept every command of our Lord, in what we believe to be its genuine import, as absolutely conclusive. The question of the use of outward ordinances is with us a question, not as to the authority of Christ, but as to His real meaning." A further statement reiterates our conviction that the baptism of Christ with the Holy Spirit is God's gracious plan to empower a believer to live a holy life, empowered and cleansed in His sanctifying power.

Intimately connected with the conviction already expressed is the view held by Friends as to the true "supper of the Lord." Again, approaching this, our attitude is intended to be affirmative, not negative. The Eucharist, mass, or communion is never to be ridiculed, but rather superseded. The presence of Christ with His church, pictured historically in the familiar Quaker painting of the *Presence in the Midst*, is not designed to be symbolic or a representation with wine or wafers, but in the real communication of His own Spirit. "I will pray the Father, and he shall give you another Comforter, that he may abide with you forever." (John 14:16 KJV) Convincing of sin, testifying of Jesus, taking of the things of Christ, this blessed Comforter communicates to the believer and to the church in a gracious, abiding manifestation, the *real presence* of the Lord. It is the remembering, the experiencing, the reality of His nearness, and His convicting yet uplifting power that worship with fellow Christians or alone enables us to under-stand the words of the apostle as expressive of the sweet and most authentic reality: "The cup of blessing which we bless, is it not the communion of the blood of Christ? The bread which we break, is it not the communion of the body of Christ? For we being many are one bread, and one body: for we are all partakers of that one bread." (1 Cor. 10:16, 17 KJV)

The Roman Catholic teaching regarding the Eucharist insists that in a process called "transubstantiation" the actual body and blood of Christ is present as one partakes of the wafer and the wine. Surgery has even been attempted to prove this! While Friends do not believe in the chemical miracle of that possibility, we do believe in the spiritual miracle of that actually happening when we are in communion worship with God. This is a sacred and vital truth to us, for without communion Friends have nothing. Our communion is partaking of the One who said "I am the Bread of Life." It is Robert Barclay who wrote, "Our communion with Christ is and ought to be our greatest work."

The basic principle of Barclay's position is that if a person has the reality, nothing else is required, and if he does not have the reality, nothing else will suffice. Robert Barclay also had the opinion that many of the churches had degenerated into the use of sacraments as a kind of religious magic. It isn't too difficult to understand what he was concerned about when one sees those frantically arranging to provide an infant ceremony of baptism when the child is sick to the point of death.

Since reference has been made to the Roman Catholic Church, it is of interest to recall that in earlier centuries the question was whether there should be seven sacraments, or two. This debate led to bitter divisions at the time of the Reformation. The arguments often turned on which ceremonies Christ had actually instituted. What Barclay, representing the Quaker view, did, was to break through this argument to a

deeper basis of inquiry. It is useless to discuss which ceremonies Christ instituted if His real purpose was to take the
church beyond ceremonies to something more fundamental.
Without getting into the question as to whether or not "do this
in remembrance of me" is accurately translated (the *Revised
Standard Version* and the *New English Bible* do not include it
except in the margin), the practical question for the Christian
is not *whether* but *how* this communion is to be effected. This
reference is made, of course, to the "last supper" of Christ
when observing the Passover Feast with His disciples. John's
Gospel in reality focuses mostly on the feet-washing act.
Relating that to the statement, "This is my body..." the ambi-
guity is apparently intended. This may mean identity, equality,
inclusion, or existence, and it should perhaps be used in the
context of another statement of Jesus when He said, "I am the
door," and in similar analogies. It is so stated in Revelation
3:20 (KJV) where the promise so wonderful to us says,
"Behold I stand at the door and knock; if any man hear my
voice, and open the door, I will come in to him, and sup with
him, and he with me." We see this as an invitation that provides hope for the entire world, including those who do not
have available any material bread and wine that has been
blessed by a priest or a religious leader. Reflecting on this
makes Robert Barclay's further observation to the Catholics
and the Anglican Church quite provocative: "Your communion
is too small."

Recalling again that much of the Book of Acts is a transition
and learning period for those first Christians, a significant
insight comes from a conclusion reached by the Jerusalem
Council reported in Acts 15. (This example will be used again
in a later chapter on decision-making.)

A serious discussion had developed, and it had to do with
the question of the use of Jewish traditions and practices in the

church. Was the Passover Feast Jesus observed with the Twelve a fulfillment of the Old Testament Law, or the establishing of a new rite for the church? Specific attention was being focused on the practice of circumcision. Hear Peter's plea:

> After much discussion, Peter got up and addressed them: "Brothers, you know that some time ago God made a choice among you that the Gentiles might hear from my lips the message of the gospel and believe. God, who knows the heart, showed that he accepted them by giving the Holy Spirit to them...for he purified their hearts by faith. Now then, why do you try to test God by putting on the necks of the disciples a yoke that neither we nor our fathers have been able to bear?...We believe it is through the grace of our Lord Jesus that we are saved, just as they are." (Acts 15:7-11 NIV)

Following this speech, Paul, Barnabas, and Silas give their reports of how the Lord is blessing in various mission fields. The final summing up of the Council's deliberation is given in verses 28 and 29 (NIV). "It seemed good to the Holy Spirit and to us not to burden you with anything beyond the following requirements: You are to abstain from food sacrificed to idols, from blood, from the meat of strangled animals and from sexual immorality. You will do well to avoid these things. Farewell."

That the practice of communion in various forms and occasions is followed in many churches suggests that it is more a cultural one than a scriptural injunction, i.e., the communion at weddings, on holidays, and selected church events. The practice may relate more to contemporary forms of worship than to an essential, just as different people and congregations seem to have different tastes in music, leadership styles, and worship atmosphere. If this is the case then one would hesitate to discourage a practice that brings blessing, much like having a choir or some other familiar worship experience. That

Friends have learned to recognize and learn the value of silent communion in reverent contemplation of the atonement of our Lord, listening to His voice within, being spiritually led and fed in the experience, is a fact deeper than culture or some religious exercise using the elements and hands.

It happens in my own experience as a missionary among a people where their major religious orientation was with a mixture of Roman Catholic and animistic beliefs the use of symbolic bread and wine was immediately identified with a meaningless past. Upon finding the Lord Jesus and His infilling of the Holy Spirit, their spiritual needs were met in a wonderful and fresh revelation of truth and reality. This experience deepened my appreciation for spiritual communion, demonstrating the danger of depending too greatly on outward forms to provide a substitute for the broken body and shed blood on Calvary.

As in the rite of water baptism, there comes the question of who is qualified to serve communion; when; and who may participate. Different denominations have various practices and conclusions, which suggests it is not clear in Scripture that it is necessary. The Reformation period is instructive in this regard, for the divisions resulted in so many interpretations. The Roman Church did not arrive at its dogma on the subject until several centuries after the church began. The earliest church seemed to combine several Jewish customs with a developing understanding of what Christian worship was to be. We believe the use of wine and wafers is more of a continuing adaptation of the Jewish passover than a command of Christ for this dispensation.

The symbolism of washing the feet, of expressing love as the mark of Christian relationships—these and other acts of Christ are more challenging to sacrifice and obedience.

An illustration comes from an earlier Friends writing. When two young people are in love, engaged to be married, they often exchange photographs, especially if they live apart for a time. Those pictures are prominently placed and often studied because of their longing for each other. But once they are married, they seldom even look at the photographs. Why should they? They see each other all the time. So with our faith. The Passover and other symbols and ordinances were used to help the Jews remember the coming Messiah. But He came! Furthermore, He has sent His Spirit to be not only with us but in us. So we can enjoy His actual presence all the time. Using only symbols or the elements can become a shallow substitute for feasting on the Bread of Life.

Chapter III
CALLED TO MINISTRY

There are different kinds of gifts, but the same Spirit.
There are different kinds of service, but the same Lord.
There are different kinds of working, but the same God
works all of them in all men.—1 Cor. 12:4-6 NIV

It is not easy to pick a Friends minister out of a crowd. There is no clerical collar, no robe, no special tone or gait; a Friends minister may be a man or woman of almost any age, with theological degrees, or with little education. Most of them are uncomfortable with a title, especially when called "Reverend." Some are quite quiet, others are loud. Some are pensive, who frown a lot, others are aggressively outgoing and laugh often. Friends ministers are as different from each other as anybody else. How then can the Friends concept of ministry be defined with any commonality or distinctiveness? Let's think about that for a while.

Mere hunting for distinguishing characteristics is hardly a worthwhile effort. There is no point in ferreting out Friends distinctives of any sort, neither finding them nor losing them, unless they grow out of the transforming experience of Christ within and become clear, convincing relevancies. The proper question to ask regarding Friends beliefs, including those relating to the ministry, is to discern if they come from an authentic, growing relationship with God that is expressed redemptively in this present world. Leaning too heavily on heritage or outward appearances can quickly become a lifeless echo, or a misleading direction.

It is reassuring to have a three-and-a-half-century past. Quakers have been around for a while. So have Friends ministers, functioning, though not elevated, as priestly personages. But even a cursory review of our history uncovers many blemishes. Legalism, pride, jealousies, coldness, poor organization, inadequate disciplines, divisions, drifting....Quakers have a tendency to write a lot, consequently the whole sad journal, minutes, and meetings of these idiosyncrasies are there for all to examine! But core convictions and the Truth of God at the center remain as bright and beautiful as ever, and God is still patiently working with this generation. Perhaps it is when we assume to have become really professional Christians (and ministers) that we become the most pathetic. God's strength is made perfect in our weakness (2 Cor. 12:9).

It must be said to the glory of God, however, that Friends testimonies are solidly based in Scripture and the witness of the Spirit, so one can find in our past the finest examples of revival, evangelism, missionary outreach, church growth, service to humanity, social concern and reforms, innovation and courage. It has been said there are in history more martyrs per capita among Quakers than any denomination since the Book of Acts.

The dignity and urgency of Friends ministry comes not from degrees or prestige, but in the humbling knowledge that God has chosen us as recorded in John 15 to be His friends! Chosen. Chosen to bear fruit, fruit that will remain. That is still happening. It is possible, now. What is needed is a fresh spiritual awareness of this, not in some historic form, or some peculiar manifestation or spectacular, esoteric fanfare exhibition, but something made to order by the Lord for our day and generation.

In spite of the trend today toward ecumenicity and religious homogeneousness as the ideal, even in the evangelical community, there is still a great need for a denominational identity, a firm, clear connection based on convictions. This allows not only for inner stability and consistency in faith and practice, it has similar values such as being a member of a family, or having citizenship in a country. Declared discipleship requires fellowship and congeniality...and in the creative plan of God, variety. God made flowers with many colors and shapes, species of unimaginable varieties. The church is not to be a monolithic mold with only one style, mode, or name. Our oneness is in Christ, not in imperceptible or labored blending of all churches into one boring mass. This is true in history.

In spite of enforced conformity, an undercurrent of change, variety, and fresh manifestation of God is found. The church is invincible—even in the dark ages, and as now seen in China.

Friends are misunderstood sometimes in the assumption one can believe anything or nothing and be an okay Quaker. This unfortunate reputation was described by Gerald Priestly in a lecture:

> ...a newcomer in our midst finds it hard to make out what we believe, if anything. One gets the impression that the average Quaker Meeting consists half of people who are resting [perhaps permanently] from the doctrinal battlefield and half of people who have smuggled in their own favorite doctrines from other churches and are quietly picnicking of them in the Meetinghouse. (Gerald Priestly, 1982, Swarthmore Lecture.)

Not true! There are certain fundamentals that characterize our yearly meetings. Our understanding of nonnegotiable
truth rests on at least three basics:

1. We come to Jesus in faith for forgiveness of sins to
   be made new persons. Christ becomes our Savior,
   our Lord.
2. We are baptized by Christ with the Holy Spirit and
   are cleansed, sanctified, directed, and empowered.
3. The process starts of learning, of nurture, witness-
   ing, teaching others (beginning with ourselves), our
   loved ones, our neighbors, and our world the word
   of peace and truth as revealed by Scripture and the
   Spirit.

Growing out of these fundamental convictions and experiences come the concepts that hold us as Friends...not so
much held, as *holding* us. Concepts regarding worship, ministry, sacramental living, peacemaking, decision-making, and
other distinctives hinge to these convictions. The result is a living faith and practice that bears for us a Quaker stamp that is
identifiable. Note, this is a result, not a goal. Our goal is to
know Christ and serve Him in this present time. This definitive
difference is important.

Choosing a church to attend, a Christian fellowship, or a
denomination can be randomly and thoughtlessly done,
selecting according to a number of superficial, even trivial
factors—the popularity of the pastor, how "exciting" or enter-
taining the programs are perceived to be, "Are my or our
needs being met?"—rather than "Is it a place to grow and
serve?" Or deciding only on one feature, such as a music program or geographical proximity, are among the shallow reasons a church is sometimes *used.*

Another factor may be added—the complexity of Christian
loyalties and attractions in the midst of a plethora of para-
church organizations competing for our attention and support
all the way from World Gospel Mission to World Vision,

including the media loaded with radio "ministries" and the "electronic" church, which is ubiquitous. Many of these are worthwhile, but are not substitutes for a home church.

Friends are not a creedal church. This bothers some, not for theological reasons, but simply because they want a quick, pre-fabricated, neat checklist of things to believe and do, which when done will handily take care of their religious responsi-bilities...mindless faith and practice. Criteria other than precise religious rules are used by Friends to determine spiri-tually acceptable conformity. "Doctrinal Standards and Friends Testimonies" fill 29 pages in our Yearly Meeting *Constitution and Discipline*. The wording of these declarations is couched in language designed to *describe* what we believe, do, and encourage. These statements are not regarded as infallible. They are guidelines; they are reworded occasionally; they are "in process" rather than cemented in.

Here is an example of one:

The pastoral gift...consists especially of the ability to do personal work with individuals or with families. This gift fits the possessor of it to comfort those who mourn, to lead the members into a deeper religious life, to arouse in the young an interest in the things of the Spirit, and to impress others with a sense of the scope and the reality of the spiritual life. It is the gift of shepherding and feeding the flock.

The church cannot make or appoint ministers, it can only recognize gifts where they exist and properly pro-vide for their exercise and development as a sacred bestowal of the Head of the Church.

Here is another:

> As it is the prerogative of the Great Head of the
> Church alone to select and call the ministers of His
> Gospel, so we believe that both the gift and qualifica-
> tion to exercise it must be derived immediately from
> Him, and that, as in the primitive church, so now also,
> He confers spiritual gifts upon women as well as men,
> agreeably to the prophecy recited by the Apostle Peter,
> "It shall come to pass in the last days, saith God, I will
> pour out my Spirit upon all flesh: and your sons and
> your daughters shall prophesy...." (Acts 2:17 KJV)
> —*Constitution and Discipline*, Northwest Yearly
> Meeting of Friends Church, 1979, pp. 24, 28

This microcosmic statement touches Friends theology on
both the calling and recording of ministers. It is an interpretation and description of what we are doing and why, rather
than a creedal statement.

Another brief comment from page 24 is noteworthy:

> ...the Gospel should never be preached for money...it
> is the duty of the church to make such provision that
> it shall never be hindered for want of it.

This implies that when a local congregation is able, it
should release a pastor to serve without insisting on a bivoca-
tional means of support.

Another device for describing our convictions is the use of
questions called "queries." These are prepared (and updated
from time to time) to serve as reminders of standards of moral
and spiritual life, which Friends seek to hold high. Not to be
used as a "letter of the law," or as disciplinary clubs, or as bar-

riers to membership, they serve as helpful admonishing reminders, bridges to understanding a relevant faith.

It is assumed that to maintain integrity as well as to expect the continual anointing of the Lord upon one's ministry among Friends, all, including pastors, tacitly if not openly affirm by convincement the major tenets of the church. One is to take seriously these doctrines and practices that find their way into our *Discipline*. These formulations represent the efforts by our forebears and approved spiritual leaders and representative bodies under the corporate guidance of the Spirit and study of the Scriptures. Forebears and leaders, of course, are fallible; so are we all. But the Holy Spirit is trustworthy.

Is there a Friends doctrine of ministry? Yes, but it is not easily defined. Not that we are muddleheaded on a concept others see more clearly; rather, the approach to determining ministry is made from a different direction than say, Catholic priests or most Protestant clergy. Throughout our history we have sought to uphold both the *universal* ministry of all Christians and the specific, *special* ministry of some. One approaches this distinction with respect but not in a sectarian way. Friends have no desire to become competitive with other denominations or the churches God is using, rather to cooperate when possible.

One must be careful at this point, and discerning. It is not as though our denomination or ministers are more wise, more clever, more spiritual than others. We have no corner on truth in that sense. Nor does a recorded Friends *minister* have more spirituality, righteousness, or fervor than other Quakers

It is Elton Trueblood who helpfully distinguishes between "status" and "function" in describing a Quaker concept of ministry. The minister simply fulfills his or her ministry as an exercise of the gifts given of God. This does not elevate one to a status position in a priestly role requiring special recognition or deference. To "function" in the pastoral ministry, for instance, as a preaching, teaching, counseling, calling, administrating task is really a full-time undertaking. So, the pastor is "released" from other time-consuming and energy-demanding

vocations to fulfill this ministry to which he or she has been
chosen of the Lord. Such a ministry as this is not designated
by special dress, clergy robes, or titles implying super spiritual
status like "Reverend." This implies a notion of ministry inconsistent with both the New Testament model demonstrated by
our Lord and as defined in servanthood.

Apostle Paul in writing the Ephesian church, and elsewhere,
mentions the several gifts given to Christians—pastors, teachers, evangelist, and others. In evaluating these, Robert Barclay
in his *Apology* (Book 10, Article 26), after arguing for the universal ministry of all, goes further: "We do believe and affirm
that some are more particularly called to the work of ministry,
and therefore are fitted of the Lord for that purpose; whose
work is more constantly and particularly to instruct, exhort,
admonish, oversee, and watch over their brethren; and
that...there is something more incumbent upon them in that
respect than upon every common believer."

Another early Quaker leader, Joseph John Gurney, also
equated these particular gifts with the New Testament gift of
prophecy consisting of "exhortation, edification, and comfort."
Consequently, Friends in most yearly meetings consider these
gifts as "recordable." Other gifts are regarded just as useful and
important when obediently exercised but usually do not
require one to give full time from other vocational pursuits.

Keeping this balance of acceptance and respect for the various gifts God gives to those in a local church is a constant
responsibility. Two factors especially are to be kept always in
mind: the identification of those gifted for the ministry and
how they are recognized, and a consistent spiritual procedure
for encouraging the development and use of the gift to ministry.

George Fox discovered a fact that needs regular *re*discov-
ery as a guiding principle for Friends when he observed "ministers are not made at Oxford and Cambridge." It takes more

than education, sophistication, and professional standing to make one a minister of the Gospel. Not that any of these are despised, but they alone are not adequate, in fact, may at times be a barrier to the most effective exercise of the God-given gift of ministry.

God at times favors and chooses the least-likely-to-succeed preachers. The Bible is filled with examples, as Howard Macy has pointed out in his writing on this subject. "Moses, the hardened stutterer shepherd; Gideon, the not-so-brave warrior hiding in a winepress; David, the youngest son least expected to be the one Samuel was seeking to anoint king; Jeremiah, who protests his youth; and, not the least of all, Jesus, the 'can-anything-good-come-out-of-Nazareth' carpenter's son." In fact, Jesus' selection of the twelve disciples was puzzling to the erudite and polished Pharisees who saw them as "ordinary" and from the wrong background, "Galilee!" Again, this point is now made not to insist that Friends should always search for the poorer prospects or recognize only those who are ill-prepared or with obvious limited abilities. Rather, we see the power of God as the crucial factor in the making of a minister as compared to mere human cleverness and personality. This includes an awareness that God chooses, and gives the gifts of ministry to anyone regardless of age, gender, race, education, or any other factor.

Linked with this distinction in discerning the gifts of ministry is the importance of alertness on the part of the local church, especially the elders, in recognizing and encouraging those so gifted. To quote again from the counsel of Joseph John Gurney:

...It is the sole prerogative of the Great Head of the Church itself, to choose, prepare and ordain, his own ministers. Man is no adequate judge before hand of the capacity of another for such work [the ministry]; and often are the individuals, only in our own wisdom, we should be prone to prefer for the purpose, passed over by the Lord.

In all this we must keep close to the specific teachings of Jesus. Returning once more to the key passage in John 15, it is important to analyze the significance of "You did not choose me, but I chose you to go and bear fruit—fruit that will last." (John 15:16 NIV) The word *you* in this statement is plural; it also has no gender designation. The call to ministry has no masculine implications in the words, the spirit, or actions of Jesus. The Lord, in His sovereign wisdom, chooses whom He will—men or women, young or older, cultured or disadvantaged, to be fruit-bearing witnesses and gifted for any ministry.

The church, through the years, and again in our generation, is under the influence of popular theological notions and cultural moods that equate ministry with masculinity. In doing this many seem to examine the Scriptures prejudicially, they do their Bible "exegesis backwards." (Arthur Roberts) This is discouraging and dishonoring to the love and grace of God. It results in a point of view that God doesn't really trust, call, use, or anoint women for ministry. Yet, a close or even a casual study of the examples, the attitude, and teachings of Jesus makes it obvious that He never treated women as inferior in any way. In doing so, He went against the customs of His time and culture, shocking even the disciples with His unconventional caring and His peer-level conversations with women. Women are coheirs to salvation. Women are coreceivers of spiritual gifts. The greatest gift of all, the Holy Spirit, fell upon all on Pentecost Day, women and men alike. The list of the spiritual gifts in 1 Corinthians, chapter 12, and in Ephesians 4, make no gender restriction or discrimination as a basis as to who may receive them.

An illustration used by others seems helpful in respect to this point. It is sometimes said that a woman is to be a wife and mother, not a doctor, a pastor, or professional person. Of course a wife is to be a mother, if she chooses, but these words *wife* and *mother* refer to *relationships*, not occupations. The male counterparts are husband and father. No one says God wants men to be husbands and fathers, not doctors, accountants, farmers, or pastors, because everyone recognizes that a man can be a perfectly good husband and father and still farm or preach.

Those uncertain about this doctrine often quote from 1 Corinthians 14:34, 35 (NASB): "Let the women keep silent in the churches; for they are not permitted to speak....If they desire to learn anything, let them ask their own husbands at home; for it is improper for a woman to speak in church." Also, the advice to Timothy (1 Tim. 2:12 NASB) is cited. "I do not allow a woman to teach or exercise authority over man." These can be lifted-out texts to bar women from having an equal function in the church, especially the ministry.

Taken out of context like that, as proof texts, makes them inconsistent with Paul's own practices and other instructions, as well as contradictory with Jesus' example and teaching. Paul did allow women to speak in church, on one occasion saying, *when they speak* they should wear their head coverings...(1 Cor. 11:5). (Only a few denominations insist on headcoverings as a literal command for all women in church.) Paul's reference relates to a specific custom and cultural situation. He was urging that meetings for worship be quiet, not noisy or disrupted with confusion, everything done "properly and in an orderly manner." To interpret the two references cited in the above paragraph as cultural matters is more consistent with Bible exegesis and teaching than to explain away all the other more complete references of Paul, or of Jesus in the Sermon on the Mount, in their entire tone and emphasis. The Bible does not contradict itself, nor of course, does Paul while addressing different situations in different churches.

There are many examples, but one is taken specifically. It is Jesus with the Samaritan "Woman at the Well." He talked with her. A woman! An additional surprise is that she is of the despised Samaritan race, and a five-times divorced woman. Yet she was forgiven, accepted, and sent (chosen) to go and witness to her neighbors, and "Many of the Samaritans from that town believed in him because of the woman's testimony."

(John 4:39 NIV) Was not that a ministry? How unfortunate if the church prevents people Jesus helps and sends out from serving because of cultural or prejudiced pride.

We are not to stand as human judges against those whom He chooses as His ministering servants. In our church there is, of course, more than three centuries of Quaker history filled with examples of women used in ministry and missionary service. It has been my privilege to have known personally at least 20 women who have been called and blessed of God in public ministry to serve as pastors, evangelists, missionaries, Bible school or seminary teachers, church leaders and administrators. This, as a denomination, is a rich heritage. There is no question for Quakers as to whether or not God uses women in the ministry. Unless we remain clear on this truth, confirmed again and again by the Spirit's approval, we may be caught up in the myopic religious legalism that, unfortunately, characterizes many segments of the church at large.

Perhaps it should be explained that this doctrine is not to be confused with a more limited, and sometimes a different radical, political feminist movement, which may be important, but in reality unrelated to the historical and biblical position of Friends regarding women in the ministry. Many issues have been raised in our nation's history, and resolved, such as women's suffrage, abolition of slavery, prison reforms, and other equal rights concerns, many from a Christian motivation; these are the outgrowth of God's wisdom in which Friends have had a part and at times were in leadership roles. There are also helpful insights relative to how the woman as pastor and preacher fills a role simultaneously of a mother and wife in church leadership responsibilities. Friends history is replete with heroic stories that must be read by each generation recounting the ways women (and men) have been used in specific ministries in public and church service.

Once the gift of ministry of a woman or man is recognized, they may then be "recorded." Our denomination does not "ordain" them, believing only God can ordain as a part of His work in calling one to the ministry. This recording is a serious responsibility of the church, with the elders involved in careful and prayerful examination. The reason for the examination is not to prevent those called from serving, but to discern the "special" callings evidencing giftedness. Persons may occasionally speak, even fluently, to edification, or engage in exhortation or give testimony to their experience, or offer vocal prayer with evidence of spiritual power without having received, necessarily, a gift of ministry (Friends *Discipline*). If the elders and the local church believe a gift of ministry is evident, that gift is encouraged and the person also urged to exercise the gift. As this ministry grows in the life of the individual so gifted, and in the life of the church as well, this is reported to the local church in a business meeting. If approved, this is communicated to the yearly meeting. A further review is made by a yearly meeting committee named to encourage the recording of those discerned to be gifted for ministry, and upon being satisfied that God has indeed chosen one for the ministry, this individual is recorded a minister of the Gospel. A manual has been prepared to guide local churches and yearly meeting committees involved, as well as the individuals themselves, in this entire process.

The recording procedure and act, in the Friends Church, is not something appropriately sought by any person, as one pursues the granting of a graduate degree or a professional diploma. Rather, the one chosen of the Holy Spirit seeks to obey and minister faithfully "as unto the Lord." It often comes as a humbling surprise to the one so chosen to realize this giftedness is special or specific. The recognition of the church is a way of showing its support, of opening doors of ministry and enabling the fulfillment of the calling. At the same time, the recording process and act is not to be done as a device to "screen" undesirable "candidates" or to impose hurdles to competency in ministry. The tender, supportive attention of the recording committee is to assure that every helpful encouragement and counsel be provided to the one called, enabling the person to be well-prepared and liberated to serve the Lord. Because of these rather delicate and unique distinctions between recording and the practice of ordination among many denominations with as many different requirements or ceremonies accompanying the designations, Friends are obliged to wait for the Spirit's direction in thoughtful reflection of the nature of spiritual gifts in maintaining a clear witness about Christian ministry.

While we have been talking mostly about the ministry of preaching, pastoring, evangelistic efforts as a full-time vocation, there *is* the ministry of every member. The church, someone has said, is not a spectator sport. We are not to be mere watchers of the church and the pastoral leadership, we are all to be workers, obedient to the Holy Spirit in our own involvement. All are to be led of the Holy Spirit; He uses each of us.

It is really rather hard to pick out the "recorded" ministers in the early church as narrated in the Book of Acts. Were Stephen, or Philip, or Dorcas ministers? Of course, but not professionally. Those today who pray, serve, tithe, are consistent in Christian living and in learning the Scriptures, God uses. Each Christian sets out under the Spirit's anointing to honor the Lord, to win others to the Lord, to bring their time, their interests, resources, and abilities under the Spirit's control. This, for us all, means constant reprioritizing all of these in devotional sensitivity. This brings a sense of personal self-worth, self-confidence, and an effectiveness in the church in the fulfillment of its intended purpose. Furthermore, the convictions being put forward now are to be carried into the minds and souls of our children and grandchildren, so that each generation will be more Christian than the last! While we are pleased to have those who find Friends for the first time as their church, it is also reassuring to see perennial Quaker names born and cultured in the Christian environment that our Sunday schools, camps, colleges, and local church families provide. This is a ministry!

The leadership opportunities of all types within our church are means of ministry under the providence of God. Again, the role of leadership, the authority and influence expected in the exercise of leadership need definition. Take for instance the leadership role of a Friends pastor. It is different from that of a school administrator, a company president, a business manager, shop foreman, or for that matter, different from the apparent perceptions of many Protestant clergy.

The character of a shepherd suggests a pastor is not one to drive or judge members of the flock. Returning to the contemporary metaphor just used, the pastor, working with volunteers and an all-amateur Christian community, cannot fire people, change the rates or the house rules, or even expel those who appear intransigent. This means in management terms the leadership style and structures in the Friends Church do not properly pyramid as they do in a secular organization or a company trying to make a profit. So the use of normal tools in organizational promotion such as offering raises, handing out rewards, fringe benefits, or grade points are not suitable. Sometimes church members, or pastors themselves, do not understand this. (This metaphorical illustration comes from Lyle Schaller.) The purpose and practice of the church works from a different principle than any other organization in society. This means caution is needed in measuring success of the church. It has been jokingly said that success in the church is determined by the "3 B's": bodies, buildings, and budgets. If enough people join and the building is beautiful and money pours in, the world regards a church as successful. That is the problem. It is the world's standards rather than God's.

Who can measure ministry, serving, obedience, or the impulses to holy living or moral insights that come in spiritual maturing? That "bottom line" belongs to God, not to any of us.

So, because spiritual results cannot be easily measured, we sometimes overlook or forget them entirely! And, unfortunately perhaps, when they *can* be measured, it is easy for us to take the credit and the glory rather than giving it to God. All leaders in this world, except pastors, are expected to be performance minded and result oriented.

Again it is Lyle Schaller who reminds us that a pastor's role changes almost imperceptibly from leader to follower. This sounds like a contradiction at first, but it needs to be understood to comprehend the nature of the ministry, indeed, of the church as well. Planning, organization, directing, budgeting, teaching, counseling, preaching, study—these describe the job of the ministry. Beyond this, a pastor is a steward of the resources of people, of money, of time, of space, and knowledge as it relates to the church especially. But notice this important distinction: one *uses* money, time, space, and knowledge, but one *develops* people. Pastoral leadership is diminished when one uses people to develop things or programs rather than to use things and programs to develop people.

The Friends ministry, of pastors and others, is to know and understand the special burdens carried by those of the congregation. Leadership under the Spirit's anointing is needed to see, communicate, and project a vision of what the church is and could become; to set the priorities, define the problems as well as the plans. The sick are to be visited, weddings and funerals conducted. The organizational life of the meeting is to be administered, fellowship encouraged, equipping others in their newly found faith and gifts—these constitute a range of expectations in the function of ministry.

Beyond this is the guarding of the Truth as known by the Friends Church, and a clear understanding of the implications of this knowledge in today's society and world. How different this is from a point of view that holds the clergy or priest in

holy reverence in a status posture. A most provocative, pointed, and challenging explanation of this is given by our Lord
Jesus:

> Jesus called them [the disciples] together and said,
> "You know that the rulers of the Gentiles lord it over
> them, and their high officials exercise authority over
> them. Not so with you. Instead, whoever wants to
> become great among you must be your servant, and
> whoever wants to be first must be your slave—just as
> the Son of Man did not come to be served, but to serve
> [minister], and to give his life a ransom for many."
> (Matt. 20:25-28 NIV)

Another definition and specific counsel comes from Paul's
instructions to the saints and pastors in the church: "To prepare God's people for works of service, so that the body of
Christ may be built up until we all reach unity in the faith and
in the knowledge of the Son of God and become mature,
attaining to the whole measure of the fullness of Christ." (Eph.
4:12, 13 NIV)

This spiritually high intensity purpose of the Great Commission in reaching the world, including the neighborhood
about us, and to make them well-trained Christians, is the specific calling of the Friends minister and the Friends Church.

Chapter IV
LETTING PEACE PREVAIL

*Make every effort to live in peace with all men and to be
holy; without holiness no one will see the Lord.*
—Hebrews 12:14 NIV

Getting even takes up the energy, time and thought of many people. We've all gone through this experience sometime or other. Maybe some are still working at it!

There is a more sophisticated word for it: retaliation. Retaliation is actually a way of life, it seems, in international relations. The waves of terrorism making daily headlines are largely a grisly checklist of how enemies try to get even. There are a few other words we use in describing this unhappy, often tragic part, of human relationships—words like feuds, retribution, revenge. On a personal level it may take the form of snubbing, refusing to speak to someone. Even failing to smile or follow the common courtesies of civilized behavior are rooted in the problem of getting even.

As Christians, this becomes a basic point of conduct. It begins within our hearts, it touches every aspect of our relationships in the home, the church, and the world. Jesus was explicit on this: "If you are offering your gift at the altar and there remember that your brother has something against you," our Lord says, apparently assuming anyone would know it is impossible for a Christian to have "something against" another believer, "leave your gift there in front of the altar. First go and be reconciled to your brother; then come and offer your gift." (Matt. 5:23, 24 NIV)

Before elaborating the subject of peace further, another helpful point is made again by Jesus in the same discourse that instructs us about how to relate, not just to a fellow Christian, but to those who are not. "You have heard that it was said, 'Eye for eye, and tooth for tooth.' But I tell you, Do not resist an evil person. If someone strikes you on the right cheek, turn to him the other also." (Matt. 5:38, 39 NIV)

More is added in this passage known as the Sermon on the Mount. At times these verses are explained as relating primarily to the Roman culture of the day. Perhaps so, but like the not-so-pious observation of Mark Twain about the Bible, "It's not the parts hard to understand that worry me, but those parts that are impossible to misunderstand that bother me!" The obvious meaning of these expressions of Jesus is unmistakable.

The seventh Beatitude (Matt. 5:9 NIV) is not to be extracted from the others as most important or as irrelevant in our lives today. "Blessed are the peacemakers, for they will be called sons of God," comes close to the authentic character of Christianity. Like all others, this Beatitude is clearly another description of Jesus Himself and of a true follower of the Lord. It is not *more* important than any other, it just is *as* important, and fits into the whole spiritual mosaic of what true Christianity is.

This leads to the observation that as a Friends Church, ours is not accurately described as simply a "peace church," but rather, a denomination that takes seriously and literally the teachings of Jesus regarding peace, as we try to do the other doctrines taught.

It needs to be said also, perhaps, that in looking at the Scriptures, especially the message of Jesus as given in Matthew's Gospel, we are not leaving the Bible to talk about politics, peace, and war. We are instead trying not to ignore those passages that teach about peace. This is part of being a "Christian" church.

To go a step further, our understanding of the doctrine of peace is tied to our Friends concept of holiness. "Make every effort to live in peace with all men and to be holy; without holiness no one will see the Lord." (Heb. 12:14 NIV) Without the power of the Holy Spirit it is impossible to consistently be either holy or peaceful.

With this deep core conviction, one can hardly imagine a more relevant teaching or truth for us to consider. These are not seen as goals, they are qualities, principles, descriptions of what Christian character really is. Someone has cynically said, "Doctrine has been the curse of the church!" No. Undoctrine, unclear teaching, fuzzy, or compromising thinking about what Jesus said and meant has been the problem.

Another reason for the relevancy of this subject is that the painful practice of retaliation and retribution is a root cause for the many marriage breakdowns, the relationship difficulties too often found in churches and within other Christian circles, to say nothing of society in general. We know this carnal tendency affects children early.

While only the glaring, bizzare, or physically injurious demonstration of retaliatory attitudes among teens and adults make the news media, there is the subtle, below-the-surface kinds of warfare that come under the scrutiny of the Scriptures. Getting even, "giving one a piece of my mind," resigning from a committee with resentment, or from other responsibilities, to get even (or using one's influence to maneuver another person out of his or hers)—these are to be considered.

It is not a new problem. It was an old problem when Jesus addressed it, not once, but many times. His hearers instantly understood just as we do what He was getting at when He talked about the system of "an eye for an eye...." Remember? Cain got even with Abel, his brother, and became the first murderer. That apparently was the first in a diabolical chain of events, a sinful system of solving differences that eventually led to the Mosaic Law as elaborated in such detail in Exodus 21, and Deuteronomy 19. "Eye for eye, tooth for tooth, hand for hand, foot for foot, burning for burning, wound for wound, stripe for stripe." (Ex. 21:24, 25 KJV) "...life shall go for life...." (Deut. 19:21 KJV)

While this principle is still prevalent in the Middle East culture and debated in the Western world, Jesus' teaching was an explanation of the church. These might be referred to as the "then" and "now" comparisons the Lord used. "It has been said, of old, an eye for an eye and a tooth for a tooth...but I tell you...[do not take revenge]." (Matt. 5:38-42 KJV) Moses was chosen to convey the governing principles for controlling excesses in outbursts of anger, violence, the urge to revenge. Surely no elaboration is needed with this all too familiar tendency to hit back. Following a slight injury, a person gets revenge. The animal fighting pattern develops "tooth and claw," but even animals seldom stoop to child or companion abuse in displays of temper. What the Old Testament Law called for was an improvement on a system that quickly degenerates into a demand for both eyes for one eye, or a whole mouthful of teeth and a broken jaw for one tooth! Exact justice is better than living in a jungle of guerilla warfare or kangaroo courts.

Jesus taught and demonstrated "a more excellent way," and on Pentecost Day baptized those who were prayerfully obedient, with the Holy Spirit, bringing power to live as [peaceful] witnesses.

The Christian is lifted to a plane, a way of life beyond human ability and inclination. "Vengeance is mine, I will repay, saith the Lord." Christian theology is beginning to take shape. Jesus said, "I am the way, the truth, and the life." (John 14:6 KJV)

The Way? The Gospel of Christ is seen by many Christians as a way *to* life. Friends insist Jesus is saying, too, that the Gospel is also a way *of* life. It is easy to miss this doctrinal distinction. Discipleship is costly as well as a way of hope, especially in a world still dominated by the retaliation principle. The way of peace is a proper alternative in spite of being often ignored and rejected in the world.

As always, the doctrines taught by Jesus are also demonstrated in the early church. The Apostle Paul puts it in clear perspective in his discourse on (Quaker?) faith and practice: "If someone has done you wrong, do not repay him with a wrong. Try to do what everyone considers to be good. Do everything possible on your part to live in peace with everybody. Never take revenge, my friends, but instead let God's anger do it. For the scripture says, 'I will take revenge, I will pay back, says the Lord.' Instead, as the scripture says: 'If your enemy is hungry, feed him; if he is thirsty, give him a drink; for by doing this you will make him burn with shame.' Do not let evil defeat you; instead, conquer evil with good." (Romans 12:17-21 TEV)

This is how peacemaking works. One wonders what a national policy of giving food to the hungry, medical care to the ill, agricultural aid and business capital to the poor would do in making for peace as compared to exporting munitions and armaments to small and larger countries. Any lasting goodwill our nation has established internationally stems from these kinds of efforts, rather than through military intervention. How sad it is that our nation now is lower on the list of generosity in goods and services to third world countries than many other less affluent nations of the world!

The principle described by Paul in writing the church at Rome in Romans 12 is apparently what the early church everywhere understood Jesus' teaching about retaliation to mean. This shows the spirit as well as defining the letter of the new law for Christians. As has been said, "God not only forgives sin, He keeps checking up on it."

The Sermon on the Mount and complete record of Jesus' teaching are more than sabbath sermons or casual talks along the roads with His disciples. They are seminar courses in behavioral theology. They are to be taken seriously, not something beyond our reach or considered irrelevant because we live in a world that doesn't accept Christ's teachings. These are not "off-the-wall" ideas of a peripheral or radical denomination. Nor are they truths to be used judgmentally, or as a threat, or to put a "guilt trip" on us or to discourage us. They are directions to show "the way." How is a Christian to act, respond, take hold of difficult situations and deal with difficult people? The world tries other ways, and so have each of us. The Christian takes another direction in his praying, in his attitudes, his actions, his motive of life. Jesus is saying that one of the best ways to see if a person is a follower of His is to watch how he reacts to unfair treatment, to unkindnesses, to other people's selfishness and terrible traits.

We find ourselves again before a New Testament teaching not unlike the matter of the sacraments, in which the church was in transition from the Mosaic legislative laws and tabernacle rituals to a new dispensation of grace. We are in the era of the Church. Our citizenship is in the Kingdom of God.

That this is difficult, even confusing, is not surprising. The Jews of Jesus' day resented His coming as a humble servant rather than as a powerful military leader. Palm Sunday dramatized this. From His birth in a manger to His vocation as a carpenter, He disappointed those wanting a different kind of ruler. His ministry, even though prophesied long before as a "suffering servant," came as a complete surprise and disappointment for many who "followed him no more" upon learning that self-denial and servanthood was His message.

It is still surprising today. And unacceptable to many. Instead of removing the shackles of persecution as the Jews longed for, Jesus told His followers persecution would actually increase. It did. At a time when they thought they were to at last gain the power to take revenge on their oppressors, they were told not to resist evil (Matt. 5:39). If they chose to be His disciples, He warned they would be arrested, flogged, cursed, hated, mistreated, ostracized, betrayed, insulted, and killed. When all these things happened to them, they were not to be surprised or even disappointed, but to rejoice (Luke 6:23). When a world sets itself to follow the principles of warfare and retaliation, this will be the normal treatment of Christians. Further, peering into the hearts of the Christians themselves, He told them even hateful, evil thoughts were as bad as murder, and that they were not to harbor contempt in their hearts (Matt. 5:22).

We believe that had Jesus chosen, He could have been a military Messiah. Satan offered Him all the world's kingdoms with all their splendor (Matt. 4:8, 9). But Jesus conscientiously objected to changing His course. He could have at almost any point become a worldly king. When Jesus spoke, everybody listened. All the reasons for a holy or a "just war" were there. Jesus knew the Romans were oppressors of victimized peoples, He knew it was soldiers that murdered infants at Bethlehem, He knew they worshiped Caesar as a false god. He knew of the sexual immorality in every major population center. He still knows all those things about our world, and we still believe God will one day rule and change everything. But our commission so clearly spelled out in His teaching is to be faithful "in the Way," until He comes. His priorities and timing remain. To divide the principles of peace between an individual mandate and a national response, or international policies, requires departure from Jesus' teaching and that of the Pauline Letters.

This is a hard truth, and frightening. It is not popular. It may account for why our church remains smaller than some. This is said in humility and sadness, not arrogantly, for nothing is more contradictory than a militant pacifism.

Let us keep close to the Scripture in this doctrine of peace. The lifestyle of the disciples was formed, and amazingly exampled in their lives after Pentecost Day along these lines (Luke 6:32-37 NASB):

> "And if you love those who love you, what credit is that to you? For even sinners love those who love them. And if you do good to those who do good to you, what credit is that to you? For even sinners do the same thing. And if you lend to those from whom you expect to receive, what credit is that to you? Even sinners lend to sinners, in order to receive back the same amount. But love your enemies, and do good, and lend, expecting nothing in return; and your reward will be great, and you will be sons of the Most High: for He Himself is kind to ungrateful and evil men. Be merciful, just as your Father is merciful. And do not pass judgment and you will not be judged; and do not condemn, and you shall not be condemned; pardon, and you will be pardoned."

Not only the twelve disciples, but the early Christians believed what He said. They lived it. Should it not be an integral truth for our church today?

It is generally agreed by most Christian scholars that the Christian church followed Christ's teachings of nonviolence for nearly three hundred years. One could quote substantiation of this at great length. Documentation is cited in *Waging Peace*, by Ralph Beebe and John Lamoreau (Barclay Press, 1980). A cursory tracing of the deviations and departure from the early church understanding of Christ's teaching regarding peace and war interests us. The concepts of "righteous" wars and "just" wars began to emerge, as Beebe and Lamoreau point out, and became a significant influence on the church under Augustine. "Do not think that it is impossible for anyone to please God while engaged in active military service," Augustine said, "War must not be fought if a just cause did not exist, but when war is undertaken in obedience to God, who could rebuke, or humble, or crush the pride of man, it must be allowed to be a righteous war."

So the just war theory became an interpretation as an "allowed" part of Christianity. This concept contributed to the Catholic pursuit of the Great Crusades. In 1095 Pope Urban II determined to unite Christendom in a war against the Moslems. "You will go forth, through the gift of God and the privilege of St. Peter, absolved from all your sins...all who die will enter the kingdom of heaven. It is in truth God's will! And let these words be your war cry when you unsheath your swords against the enemy. You are soldiers of the cross...."

This pronouncement has been used repeatedly in each generation as the Christian allowance for soldiering and warfare.

At the time of the Crusades and during many centuries since, the populace by and large were unable to study the Scriptures for themselves. Certainly the ready access to Bible teaching, Christian books and literature was not known by those who marched off to war unfamiliar with the actual teachings of Christ. Given the hierarchial structures of the church, then and now, in many cases, laity and church members assumed their Christian conduct largely on the basis of tradition or clerical pronouncements. We now, of course, have ample opportunity to search the Scriptures and seek the wisdom of the same Holy Spirit who gave them.

It may have been Martin Luther who established the position of deterrence as a Christian means of peacekeeping. [Note: peacekeeping and peacemaking are two different concepts.] Luther considered war necessary to keep peasants' obedience and to maintain peace. "The hand that wields the sword and kills with it is not man's hand, but God's; and it is not man, but God who hangs, tortures, beheads, kills, and fights. All of these are God's works and judgments...." (*Waging Peace*)

Oliver Cromwell's Puritan armies killed thousands of Catholics using basically the same point of view as "a righteous judgment of God on those barbarous wretches...." His army was issued the first "Soldier Pocket Bible."

Meanwhile, the Puritans in America, as Ralph Beebe reports, were thanking God for sending smallpox, which killed hundreds of Indians and made it easier for the Christians to take possession of the new world. When more Indians were in the way and "God" failed to send another smallpox epidemic, the Puritans did the killing. "God," they said, "was commander in holy wars against Roman Catholics, the Church of England, the Indians, Quakers, and infidels."

The same dichotomy persists. In the War of 1812, U.S. Naval Commander Stephen Decatur coined the phrase used at times since when he exclaimed: "Our country; in her intercourse with foreign nations may she always be in the right; but our country, right or wrong." World War I found Kaiser Wilhelm explaining Germany's entrance into the war by saying, "We are inspired by the unalterable will to protect the place God has set for ourselves and all coming generations...with a clear conscience and a clean hand, we take up the sword."

Often the notion is expressed in the Christian community that a literal response to this teaching of Jesus ignores the sinfulness of human nature. If everyone were perfect, then Jesus' teaching would work, but in the *real* world it won't. This position is really quite strange for a Christian to take. If everyone were perfect, then pacifism, and the Good News of the Gospel itself from which the commands to love the enemy and turn the other cheek come, would be unnecessary.

The path of peace as taught by Jesus is precisely the way to live in the sinful world where violence is so near. This brings one to grips with the injustice found in a sinful world, enabling one in the power of the Holy Spirit to witness to a deeper truth that can lead us out of darkness into the Light and Love of God. The Sermon on the Mount is not just a set of idealistic words, it is practical advice on how to live and witness in a very real world.

The question continues. The appeal and national loyalties in love of our country that we surely all feel is measured thoughtfully with the Christian teachings and attitude of the Gospel taught by Jesus. One's judgment is prayerfully made, not just on the basis of the horror of what nuclear war with the present weapons could do. What is right is the changeless truth of God regarding His plan for Christians in a world. We are to be "blameless and pure, children of God without fault in a crooked and depraved generation, in which you shine like stars in the universe as you hold out the word of life...." (Phil. 2:15 NIV)

Black leader John Perkins, founder of the Voice of Calvary Ministries in Mississippi, writes of his experiences while being severely beaten by State Police officers. "Some of my people were saying, 'Fight back! Use violence! Arm for revolution....' But I knew that God's justice is seasoned with forgiveness. Forgiveness is what makes His justice redemptive. Forgiveness!" (*A Quiet Revolution,* a publication of the VOC Ministries)

But not all Christians and denominations see it this way. Some make nationalism a Christian obligation. This is another reason for the writing of this book, attempting to enable us to identify the core convictions holding us as Friends. Rather than extending further the political or international arguments of peacemaking, or looking at the departures from Christ's teaching as originally held by all in the early Church, we surely must return to the moorings of our fundamental understanding of truth. It comes back again to the concept that Christianity is a way *of* life as well as the way *to* life. "We preach Christ." (1 Cor. 1:23 NIV) We take in trust the statement of Jesus that "all power is given to me in heaven and on earth." This is our only adequate answer to the nuclear threats, or the divisions in the church, or the fragmenting of families. Jesus, the "Prince of Peace," as seen by Isaiah, and the "Lamb of God," as seen by John, is our hope and our Peace. Paul saw Christ as the reconciler of *all* things "making peace through his blood, shed on the cross." (Col. 1:20 NIV)

Connecting the concept of peace with the doctrine of holiness and the call to evangelism is a truth that is clearly seen. Peace and evangelism go together just as "follow peace...and holiness, without which no man shall see the Lord" go together. These indicate an internal reorientation of life toward the service of others and the glory of God. Salvation replaces alienation with reconciliation, hate with love, wickedness with righteousness. The penitent have their sins forgiven; this is one of the nonnegotiable truths. It is then that our lives are set upon imitating Christ. In the body of Christ, it is our task to bring this truth along with others to the attention of those new in the faith. It is important to conscientiously work our way through this teaching until we are clear on it. This may mean reading and studying the large amount of writing, including some of the Christian classics. If, after this is done, one finds it impossible to accept the interpretation of Scripture on this matter of peacemaking, it may be best to find a fellowship that conforms to another point of view. There are certain aspects of Friends doctrine upon which there is a great liberty of conscience, but this is hardly one of them, since this so closely touches our understanding of the work and power of the Holy Spirit in holy living. God describes Himself with one word: God is love. This is central to our understanding of the Gospel.

The heartrending changes this doctrine brings to our concept of Christian faith and practice cannot be minimized. These are difficult questions. Perhaps a word of personal testimony is appropriate. As a conscientious objector to war in World War II, I remember vividly the pressures of taking such a position. There are no pat answers to the political solutions required, but one must come back to one's relationship with Christ. Can one be responsible for taking the life of another? Especially in a war where often those killed, maimed, or injured are as innocent as you? Living outside the United States for a number of years has given a depth of patriotism and love for the values of the freedoms and blessings enjoyed not previously realized. Beyond this are the implications regarding consistency in the paying of war taxes, participating in military-related industries and all the involvement in a society not governed entirely by Christian principles.

The church is not to set rigid standards of detailed responses to any of these factors, rather, only urge waiting on the Lord in the spirit of obedience in seeking His guidance in our Christian living. Some, with clear conscience, take a different position from others. We are not to sit in judgment, but accept and pray for all who are trying to honestly serve the Lord.

It has been my responsibility to stand before Selective Service draft boards with others required to respond to questions like, "What would you do if your home were attacked and your mother or sister raped? Would you stand by and let your family be murdered?" My only response is that I do not know, I can only trust in the Lord to give strength when needed. Certain experiences as a missionary came close to some of these dreaded threats, and the peace of God was precious and powerful. Other missionaries have been killed, too. It is terribly important, of course, that one's response come from Christian faith, not cowardice.

It becomes more apparent in our day that we and our nation do well to order our lives by Christian principles and truth. Both sin and virtue are very abstract terms, however. Consequently sins have at times to be written in specific ways. They got this kind of treatment in the Old Testament: unclean language, abuse of holy days, disrespect for parents, killing, adultery, stealing, lying, false witness. Turning to the New Testament one finds the Apostle Paul's list of sins is familiar to the church: fornication, impurity, indecency, idolatry and sorcery, quarrels, contentious temper, envy, fits of rage, selfish ambition, party intrigues, jealousies, drinking bouts, orgies, and the like (Gal. 5:19, 20). God's spokesmen across the years from Jeremiah to John the Baptist have been specific.

The questions facing the church today in seeing the letter and sensing the spirit of Jesus' teaching are whether or not the list of evils is complete and consistent. They do not always appear so clearly in the Old Testament, but the coming of Christ, as prophesied, seems to have made clearer the intent and plans of God for all mankind. Given the mentality of a larger segment of the evangelical church today in the strong nationalistic spirit, one is taken back to the Word and witness of Christ. There is a better way to express our patriotism than depending on the might of military missiles; certainly there is a better way to express our faith than to try to "get even" in personal and church relationships. "The gospel of peace and the power of God" are meaningful realities to put into our way of life.

A peacemaker is one about whom two things can be said: first, he thinks as a Christian, Christlike. This means a loving bias, a mentality of openness to God and loving one's neighbor...and enemies. To be this sort of person first requires one to have a new view of himself or herself, for only with a pure heart united and cleansed can one qualify. Isn't this the problem often? What will this do to me? My rights? My happiness? My family? Is this fair to me? In these reactions are found the ingredients of warfare. The peacemaker is one daily mastered by the Lord. We don't have to ask anymore why things are like they are in the world. We know. "The spirit that now worketh in the children of disobedience" is in control.

Second, the peacemaker has not only a new view of himself, but a new view of the world. This becomes the peacemaker's concern, not just to work for peace, but to see God glorified in the world. This happens in any number of ways. It comes about in fulfilling the Great Commission by "teaching them to observe all that I have commanded." And this is possible, only possible, as "You will receive power when the Holy Spirit comes on you." (Acts 1:8 NIV) It is only with His presence and power that any of the Beatitudes become living realities. This is our position as a doctrinal tenet. We are not talking about a political philosophy, or good resolutions, or even admirable character training. Our convictions come from the work of the Holy Spirit in the baptism of a heart cleansed, supernaturally, miraculously by the blood of Christ.

There is a Quaker expression that "there is that of God in every man." While the viewpoint that all are good and need only to have that spark of goodness fanned into life falls far short of the need for a spiritual rebirth, it is yet true that we recognize the sacredness of human life in every human being. There is something given in the image of God that we dare not destroy in ourselves or others. And to destroy another or despise ourselves prevents the possibility of finding God and the fullness of His redemptive plan.

"Let the peace of Christ rule in your hearts" (Col. 3:15 NIV) is our greatest privilege day by day. The beauty of this truth is that God is at work in our hearts as well as in our minds. To say that this doctrine or emphasis is too much for me, I am not able, is to answer correctly! It is at this point that we give ourselves to the Lord to let Him do in us and to us only what He can do.

"Peace be with you, all."

Chapter V
GETTING THE SENSE
OF THE MEETING

It is a little like the mechanical equipment in my car, or refrigerator. Not much attention is paid to it until something goes wrong, then one becomes suddenly aware of how important it is that it work! The routine ways of maintenance care are important, too, and often when neglected it is discovered that the mechanical malfunctionings are traceable to either neglect or something "in there" being worn out.

When the church is "functioning" well, growing, working, and worshiping in harmony, not much attention is paid to how the "business meeting" is handled. There may be curious questions on the part of newcomers, especially those who happen to come from another denomination that conducts church business quite differently, or from one who is active in the life of community organizations that make Robert's Rules of Order a useful and necessary tool. But what is taken for granted by many in the conduct of business may become suspect or abused when a "big" decision arises in the church—like changing pastors, entering a building program, or in budget planning. Suddenly the focus of attention is on how we decide about these matters, and on the reasons for the Friends "system" in the local or denominational decision-making process.

Is this a doctrine? Is it useful? Practical? Right? Or is it simply an anachronistic curiosity of Quakers that is worn-out or impractical? We don't take votes as a normal practice, we don't make motions and have them seconded in a church business session, we don't campaign for offices...and we use several expressions that sound like a meaningless foreign language such as "getting the sense of the meeting," "approved," or take time waiting without words in reflection on a matter until the "clerk" (chairman) apparently decides the issue is settled and says so. It can be confusing for those unfamiliar with the procedure. It can be frustrating if perceived as not working well when something "goes wrong," which is another way of describing disunity in the church body.

To approach this subject positively it is important to center attention first, not on the lack of Robert's Rules of Order, but rather, on certain basic concepts of what the church really is. How does it differ from other organizations in which we are involved? Why? This is quite different from trying to determine why *we* are different. Like other distinctives examined, it isn't as though Friends try to be unique as some kind of goal; it is, instead, a practicing response to a scriptural interpretation of truth discerned in examining how the church is designed in the New Testament.

So, let's step back a moment to look at the Church, not just at Friends as a denomination. The *Church* is unlike any other organization or agency. It has a unique purpose for existence. "I will build my church" (Matt. 16:18 KJV), Jesus declared, addressing Peter and the other disciples. Volumes have been written as to whether the church of that statement was to be built on Peter himself or on a faith expressed by Peter: "You are the Christ, the Son of the living God." Friends share the conviction, with other Protestants, that the church is built on the Christ Peter acknowledged. This is a deep truth that is sacred and eternal. This means that one's approach to the purpose and functioning of the Church is done reverently, prayerfully, never capriciously or casually.

The organized church utilizes the people and the methods of society in general but is founded upon a spiritual foundation. Everything that happens in the life of the church springs out of worship, our interaction and the guidance of God through the Holy Spirit. Decisions, action, worship, business sessions, all ministries of whatever nature will be under the guidance of Christ and the empowering of His Spirit.

In practical terms this means, then, that pastors, clerks, committees, decisions, and programs are spiritually inspired under the leadings of the Lord. Given this premise it brings a specific approach to how decisions, small or larger (in our viewpoint, although all decisions may be spiritual in nature), come about under the guidance of the Spirit. How are these discerned? Is this best done by majority votes or in utilizing democratic government procedures? Or is there another, better way?

It has already been explained that the pastor, or any other person in the church, is a minister, serving as gifted of the Lord to honor Him and live a life of loving concern for others. No one has autocratic powers. Each Christian is privileged to speak in worship as led of the Spirit, although some are especially gifted to preach, or teach, or administrate as opportunity is provided. The same is true in a meeting where business decisions are being made. The expression "meeting in worship for the conduct of business" describes this. All actions taken become an extension of the worship experience.

To see how this happens, it is most helpful to look carefully at how decisions were made by the church in the Book of Acts. It may be well to remember that the Christian community then developing was functioning long before Robert's Rules of Order were put together! The church's model is not the "town hall," or any similar system, even though these work well of course in fulfilling the purposes for which government or group action is necessary in most organizations. There are those, however, who have experimented with a "consensus" approach to decision-making in secular organizations, believing this often brings less divisiveness and more freedom in the exchange of ideas.

One marvels at the "power" of the early church. It came not from the usual "power structure" model with which we are familiar, but from the power of God over all. When the church is in complete agreement with one another and with the Holy Spirit, there is scarcely anything it cannot do. The work of the Lord becomes a testimony of beauty, love, and power.

By contrast, consider the havoc and hurt that comes when God's people argue (fight!) in church. If disagreements and individuality conflicts are present when issues are to be decided, these can be brought under the control of the Holy Spirit and blended into unanimous agreement through His guidance. Divisions, discord, "party spirit," however slight, threaten church stability and harmony. In a climate of disunity, all kinds of problems arise. The "flock" is vulnerable, sometimes devastated by the enemy, when a church is ruled by either majorities or minorities rather than a sense of oneness in the Spirit. Seeing that human methods divide congregations, splinter fellowships, and alienate Christians, can they be trusted as being God's plan for decision-making in the church?

Not just Quakers have found the church is not to operate like a business or managed as a branch of government. *Moody Monthly* magazine recently carried an article by a Baptist pastor titled, "Stop the Voting—You're Wrecking My Church!" He insists God provides a better way. By precept and example, God has designed another pattern for guiding His church that became the established procedure for moving forward in unity and outreach in the New Testament.

Another contemporary example of this is found in a Community Church near Portland, Oregon, which has grown to nearly a thousand with several branch churches. The pastor announced in a Church Growth Conference: "We've learned more from the Quakers than anyone else as to the secret of church unity and growth. We never take a vote in our business sessions. We wait until we are guided in total unity by the Spirit of the Lord." He pastored this church more than 25 years.

Unity is more than a mere ideal. Harmony in a church is more than excitement over a new experience. It reflects the Spirit of the Lord in the midst, for wisdom and light come from Him. It must be clearly said, of course, that it is not the "system" that brings unity, it is the Lord. And, a system of not voting that is not submitted to the Spirit in humility and obedience by all involved still fails to release the power and love characterizing the early church, or any church at its best.

The so-called democratic process is preferred in civil government over a dictatorship. But in the church, our "dictator" is a benevolent, all-wise, tender, understanding One who uses human instruments and abilities to accomplish His purpose as human, finite followers are under His leadership. A truly democratic procedure requires at least a two-party system. This cannot be seriously proposed as a good model for a local church, even though it has been often tried.

Voting, then, is an invitation to division. Whenever a vote is taken, someone loses. Is this good? The secret ballot plan, assumed by some as being the ultimate way for an honest expression of the people, simply allows for anonymity, not unity. When that procedure is followed in the church, discerning and sensitive Christians often return to their homes confused, sometimes sickened, by what they have experienced. This is not a good substitute for following the Spirit's leadings.

No doubt some reading this who have been many years in the Friends Church are thinking, well, that isn't the way it is in our church even though we have tried decision-making without voting. It must be recognized that automatic non-voting is not the answer either! There is a deeper spiritual principle to be discovered. One might also observe that many marriages do not seem to be working well either, but it is not the idea of marriage that is at fault, rather, the marriage is not being properly practiced by the partners.

It has been stated that, in the Quaker church, two kinds of assemblies are believed to be desirable: meetings for worship, which concern *being*, and meetings for the transaction of business, which concern *doing*. What is implicit in worship becomes explicit in action. The strategy of Friends organizational procedure is designed to funnel individual Christian concerns and testimonies upward, that is, from the person through the local church, to the yearly meeting, and to the world as it may be appropriately attempted. This, obviously, is quite different from a strictly followed "hierarchical system." When only the authority of a person, or of a unanimous group decision, is recognized, the supremacy of even a majority over a minority is completely dispensed with. What is really desired is to discern the will of God. And God is not divided. Voting or politicking only exposes the extent of a division on an issue.

Before analyzing further the specific ways in which the Friends business meeting functions, it is interesting to discover how the procedure developed historically. At first, the Quaker meetings for worship in which business-like decisions were made was to care for the poor, the sick, and the imprisoned. Committees were named, funds collected, and plans acted upon to handle these matters...not in a different time or place, but right out of or in the worship together. The same principle is still in effect in caring for the affairs of the church, but of course, it is more complex if not so intimately tragic as in other times. Financial reports, accounting, committee action, departmental planning, and budgeting for missions, evangelistic efforts, youth ministries, music programs, social concerns—in fact, the whole spectrum of a well-organized church is reviewed and promoted in a spirit of worship (in session) dedicated to the conduct of business. This model is used by local church administrative committees as well as in other committees. This basic philosophy and operating principle of a deep spiritual awareness through simultaneous individual and group dependency on the Spirit's leadings is a practice and heritage held in sacred trust.

"Our meetings for Church affairs ought not be business left to the few. They are intended to be gatherings in the Spirit of Christ to the whole Membership." This is a quote from one of George Fox's letters to William Penn. Penn himself stated: "There is no one who presides after the manner of the assemblies of other people; Christ only being their president, as He is pleased to appear in wisdom in any one or more [members]...to arrive at a firm unity of conviction...." In 1725 Quaker Thomas Chalkley wrote, "Considering the government of the Church of Christ, of which church he is the holy head and lawgiver...we are to seek and wait for counsel and wisdom from him in all our monthly and quarterly meetings for the well-being of our [Quaker] Society...Christ's Spirit must govern Christ's Church." Again, George Fox seems to sum it up in saying, "Friends are not like a company of people about town or parrish business, but [are] to wait upon the Lord." (From George Fox's *Journal,* and William Penn's writings in *Some Fruits of Solitude.*)

More important than Quaker history are the examples in decision-making observed in Scripture. How this works in the early church as shown in the Book of Acts and elsewhere merits our careful study. Surely these are not too idealistic or lofty for us today; rather, they are perceived as the norm for developing strategy and programs.

Consider the following: "I appeal to you, brothers, in the name of our Lord Jesus Christ, that all of you agree with one another so that there may be no divisions among you and that

you may be perfectly united in mind and thought." (1 Cor.
1:10 NIV)

The Apostle Paul encourages the same when writing
another church: "Make every effort to keep the unity of the
Spirit through the bond of peace." (Eph. 4:3 NIV) "Be perfect,
be of good comfort, be of one mind, live in peace; and the God
of love and peace shall be with you." (2 Cor. 13:11 KJV)
"Finally, all of you, live in harmony with one another; be sympathetic, love as brothers, be compassionate and humble."
(1 Peter 3:8 NIV)

These repeated exhortations to "harmony," being "perfectly united in mind," "all of you agree," "be of one mind," did not
happen coincidentally, nor quickly. One observes unhurried
waiting in prayer until these descriptions were able to be accurately accomplished. So often today, only brief "opening
prayers" are used in the discussion of business meetings.
When so much is at stake in being sure of complete unity and
harmony, a proper prioritizing of time to allow for waiting on
the Lord is always in order. It is sometimes easier to simply
appoint a committee to bring a recommendation or to vote on
a decision. While the naming of a task force or study committee is often a suitable procedure, this should never become a
trade-off for finding God's will. Spiritual work is best done in a
spiritual way. This is the point. Methods adapted or borrowed
from the world, without the seal of God's approval upon them,
are never as satisfactory as a spiritual approach.

Before examining some specific scenarios of decision-making
as precedents in the New Testament church, we will glance at
the traditional format generally followed in a Friends meeting
for business.

The presiding clerk, after a period of worship, not just a
"quickie" devotional or a few moments of silence, but adequate opportunity given to "centering down" in a spirit of communion—the clerk will bring before the meeting an agenda of

matters to be considered. The agenda is normally open-ended for review or additions. Time is permitted for careful consideration in which all members who feel concerned may express a judgment and may be heard. It is appropriate to insist that everyone speak or respond in some way, even if they have no specific concern on the subject so that Friends will know that they have no concern on the matter. If, in the course of the meeting, the clerk should discern too much time is taken in unproductive arguments, he or she may call for a waiting period before the Lord, or for postponement of a decision. When it appears to the clerk that the meeting has reached an agreement, he or she states clearly what appears to be "the sense of the meeting." If the members then give approval to the clerk's statement by simply saying "approve" or a nod of the head, a minute is written and read before the meeting. Care is subsequently taken to make certain those who are involved in the actions taken, and who may have been absent from the meeting at the time the decision was made, are made aware of the actions approved.

The degree of unity necessary for a decision depends somewhat on the importance of the question and the character and depth of feeling of those who appear to oppose (or are "uneasy" with) the general trend of the opinions expressed. On many items of routine business, little or no expression is necessary. Even silence may give consent. But on more important matters, care is taken to secure the full participation of all who are present.

An opposing minority, however small, is not disregarded. The "weight" of a member in determining the decision of the meeting depends on the confidence the meeting has in the validity of his or her judgment. On different subjects certain Friends are more knowledgeable than others. On a financial problem, the opinion of a single financier might determine the sense of the meeting, although his or her opinion might carry less weight on another subject. God uses the expertise of any disciple if this is dedicated to Him through the life and work of the church.

If an individual lays a concern before the meeting, much depends on the degree to which the concern has gripped him or her. If the concern is held deeply or perhaps is brought up again and again in spite of previous inaction or even opposition, the meeting may finally acquiesce even though a degree of hesitation was felt at first by some.

If a serious difference of opinion exists on a subject that cannot be postponed, decision may be left to a smaller committee. Not infrequently the minority withdraw their opposition in order that the meeting may come to a decision. It is, however, surprising how often real unity is reached, even though the discussion in its initial stages shows a wide variety of opinion or pronounced division.

If the Quaker method of arriving at unity does not succeed, the difficulty is generally due to the participation of some members who have not achieved the right attitude of mind and heart. Dogmatic persons who speak with an air of finality or assume the tone of a debater determined to win may be a serious hindrance. Eloquence to appeal only to the emotion is out of place. Those who come to meeting not so much to find the Lord's will as to win acceptance of their own opinions may find their views carry little weight. Opinions should always be expressed humbly and tentatively in the realization that no one person sees the whole truth and that the entire meeting, as the Body of Christ, can see more accurately than one person can see any one part of it.

It sometimes works this way: when Smith speaks following Jones, he takes into consideration Jones's opinion. Brown may follow with a statement that would probably have been different had Smith and Jones not spoken. Every member credits every other sincere member with at least some insight. Finally, a decision is made that receives the approval of all. A number of persons then say, "I approve," "I agree," or some equivalent expression. The result is more than mere group dynamics or courteous dialogue, although the Spirit may use both.

The ideal of all business discussions is to reach unified action as a sense of the Holy Spirit's leading. If this can be found without division and in a warmth of spiritual guidance, the ideal is realized.

This method does not result in a compromise. A compromise is not likely to satisfy anyone completely. The objective of the Quaker method of business is to discover the will of God, which if recognized and accepted will satisfy everyone more fully than did any position previously held. Everyone can then say, "That is what I really wanted, but I did not realize it." This approach in decision-making attempts to produce synthesis of action and concern in which each part makes some adjustment to the whole, and as in all life the whole is more than the sum of its parts. A new insight emerges through the search for the Lord's direction, and when the meeting becomes a unit in this single purpose, the answer is found. This is an achievement. Every partial, fragmentary view contributes to the total view. The new member is encouraged to study this plan and to learn by the preparation of a humble heart and prayerful thought how to contribute effectively and cooperatively in the fruitful search for God's will in the affairs of the church.

The attainment of this type of unity within the church is not the same thing, however, as uniformity. Unity is spiritual; uniformity is mechanical. For this reason it should be difficult, and often is, to discover a *distinctive* image of the Friends Church. You see, we are all individuals determined to exercise the gifts of God in the unique personalities given us, and the individual initiative that comes from God.

With this run-down on Quaker business meeting "how-to's" and "whys," let's turn to some fascinating, breathtaking New Testament case histories in working through tough church decisions. Here is one. A dilemma has developed (a problem to solve): two conflicting doctrinal opinions from two groups of

Christians who are both positive they have God's revealed truth. It is not just Smith vs. Jones, but both Smith and Jones insisting they are speaking for God, and who can argue with that? Round one has been a heated debate by which each side tried unsuccessfully to convince the other side of its errors. There was only one way out of this deadlock; they had to go down to "Yearly Meeting" at Jerusalem for a decision. (We are indebted to Charles A. Beals for this example, first prepared as a paper for a Friends ministers' gathering, and later printed in the *Evangelical Friend,* July 1982.)

The Book of Acts 15:1-3 (NIV) sets the stage:

> Some men came down from Judea to Antioch and were teaching the brothers: "Unless you are circumcised according to the custom taught by Moses, you cannot be saved." This brought Paul and Barnabas into sharp dispute and debate with them. So Paul and Barnabas were appointed, along with some other believers, to go up to Jerusalem to see the apostles and elders about this question. The church sent them on their way, and as they traveled through Phoenicia and Samaria, they told how Gentiles had been converted. This news made all the brothers very glad.

This is a serious situation. Some Jewish Christians were sent out from Jerusalem to advise the Antioch Christian brothers that they have been deluded and are consequently spiritually lost, for salvation, they say, is based on both a belief in Christ *and* circumcision according to the teaching of Moses. How can this difference in theology be resolved by a meeting of minds without compromising biblical truth or loyalty to Christ? When men as strong as Paul and Barnabas, with missionary zeal, disagree with others just as zealous, the harmony of the church is surely threatened.

Further analysis of the argument brings the conclusion that both agree one must believe in Christ to be saved, and that circumcision alone could not assure salvation. That is good and step one toward a solution. Another favorable factor is that both groups apparently earnestly wanted the will of the Lord, and also wanted both Jews and Gentiles to be saved. You see, even in what appears to be a terrible impasse, many points of unity can be found as beginning steps toward resolving differences.

Returning to the story as it unfolds in the following verses, one gets the impression an assembled meeting has been called:

> When they came to Jerusalem, they were welcomed by the church and the apostles and elders, to whom they reported everything God had done through them. Then some of the believers who belonged to the party of the Pharisees stood up and said, "The Gentiles must be circumcised and required to obey the law of Moses." (Acts 15:4-5 NIV)

The returning missionaries are making their reports. As the meeting progressed, an organized faction of the church, which in all likelihood had sent the delegation to Antioch, consisting of Pharisees who had become believers, became so incensed and disturbed that they made a public protest. They declared that the Gentiles, even believers, could not be saved without first being circumcised.

Now we come to the nitty-gritty of decision-making. Whether or not that public meeting closed in an uproar, the record does not say; but it was evident to everyone that this matter must be settled, so a business meeting was called.

> The apostles and elders met to consider this question. After much discussion, Peter got up and addressed them: "Brothers, you know that sometime ago God made a choice among you that the Gentiles might hear from my lips a message of the gospel and believe. God,

who knows the heart, showed that he accepted them by giving the Holy Spirit to them, just as he did to us. He made no distinction between us and them, for he purified their hearts by faith. Now then, why do you try to test God by putting on the necks of the disciples a yoke that neither we nor our fathers have been able to bear? No! We believe it is through the grace of our Lord Jesus Christ that we are saved, just as they are."

The whole assembly became silent as they listened to Barnabas and Paul telling about the miraculous signs and wonders God had done among the Gentiles through them. (Acts 15:6-12 NIV)

So now the business meeting is being held. "The whole assembly" was there. The meeting began with debating. *Phillips* has it "after an exhaustive debate"; the *Revised Standard Version* says there was "much debate." The *Jerusalem Bible* has it "after the discussion had gone on a long time." Reading between the lines, strong opinions are being expressed on both sides, only to achieve a stalemate.

It is almost humorous, certainly surprising, that during all this lengthy discussion, Peter apparently had not said a word! That too must have been the work of the Holy Spirit! He too was listening, meditating, waiting, and looking to the Lord for wisdom. At last he stands to his feet. The whole assembly listens. Without further argument or debate, Peter comes through simply with a fact and a deduction. The fact: as everyone present knew, he was commissioned by God to preach to the Gentiles (Cornelius was one), and in so doing had seen uncircumcised men filled with the Holy Spirit. The deduction: it is solely through the grace of our Lord Jesus Christ that Gentiles as well as Jews are saved. No rituals, no ceremonies, no former laws of the past now apply.

Following Peter's remarks anyone in the "whole assembly" had the opportunity to speak. None did. They "became silent." The impression is given that this was quite extraordinary.

What must they (all) have been thinking? These explanations of Peter make sense. I find a response in my own heart. They have the ring of divine wisdom."

Barnabas and Paul then tell of case after case where God reveals His approval of their ministry that the Gentiles can be saved solely through faith in Jesus Christ without benefit of the rites, ceremonies, or Jewish customs of any sort.

We pick up the next scene:

When they finished, James spoke up: "Brothers, listen to me. Simon has described to us how God at first showed his concern by taking from the Gentiles a people for himself. The words of the prophets are in agreement with this, as it is written:

'After this I will return
   and rebuild David's fallen tent.
Its ruins I will rebuild,
   and I will restore it,
that the remnant of men may seek
      the Lord,
   and all the Gentiles who bear my
      name,
says the Lord, who does these
      things'
that have been known for ages.

"It is my judgment, therefore, that we should not make it difficult for the Gentiles who are turning to God. Instead we should write to them, telling them to abstain from food polluted by idols, from sexual immorality...." (Acts 15:13-20 NIV)

James, the spokesman now, the clerk of the meeting, has put into words what has become the sense of the meeting. They were united. No debating now. Following Barnabas's and Paul's speeches the entire assembly again remained silent, including the Hebrew sect who had previously spoken quite vehemently in opposition to the views now expressed. No need to vote, all that was now needed was someone to put into words what the evident will of the Lord was. James did.

Another significant decision followed, made by "the whole church":

> Then the apostles and elders, with the whole church, decided to choose some of their own men and send them to Antioch with Paul and Barnabas. They chose Judas (called Barsabbas) and Silas, two men who were leaders among the brothers. With them they sent the following letter....Greetings....It seemed good to the Holy Spirit and to us not to burden you with anything beyond the following requirements.... [These were reiterated again, as noted above.]
>
> The men were sent off and went down to Antioch, where they gathered the church together [in a business meeting of worship] and delivered the letter. The people read it and were glad for its encouraging message. (Acts 15:22-31 NIV)

In a rerun of the whole story we see what has actually taken place. What if a vote had been demanded and taken at any point early in the debate and discussion? What if James, who was leading the meeting, had given in to the pressure of the time element and decided to make an arbitrary ruling just to get on with the agenda? What would that have done, not only to the church at Jerusalem, but also to the Christian Church at Antioch, perhaps impacting the church to the present day!

After waiting, after taking adequate time, the "whole church," not a two-thirds majority, not a grumbling minority, not just the pastor, but also the farmers, the workers, the housewives, *everybody* felt clear in the decision reached.

One more point is critically important. The record continues: "It seemed good to the Holy Spirit and to us." It was not enough just to have a majority, nor even to have a 100 percent agreement unless the Holy Spirit placed His seal of approval upon the actions and decisions made.

It takes more than consensus. The Holy Spirit blesses and empowers when *complete* unity is achieved. Also, the entire deliberation was carried on in a context of worship. They listened to God as He spoke to the corporate body.

One further observation on this whole development. The final decision was not precisely what either side had been saying. The decision was neither, "All Gentiles must keep the Law of Moses," nor "No Gentile needs to keep the Law," issues over which the two groups were in conflict. The choice of circumcision was just that, a choice, with the admonition made to satisfy the sensitive consciences of the Pharisee faction, namely to abstain from blood and from things strangled plus a clear instruction not previously mentioned but which all understood to be right—sexual immorality is not a Christian practice in any circumstances.

Other examples as specific of group actions through the same process just described are found in Acts chapters six and thirteen.

In a summary analysis of these precedents in Scripture, several conclusions can be drawn:

1. The congregational form of government was used exclusively in small and larger decisions.
2. The apostles and elders acted as advisors and guides in their leadership roles, but did not function as bishops or with authoritative control. The voices of "weighty mem bers" like Peter, Barnabas, Paul, and others in the Jerusalem meeting may have carried more influence than a dozen or more of the others.

3. There is no indication that voting was done. Action followed only upon 100 percent approval including the confirmation of the Holy Spirit.
4. The Holy Spirit reveals His will to a corporate group as well as to individuals within it.
5. They corroborated their decisions with the Scripture.
6. A minute of the action was prepared by the presiding officer and was read for approval.
7. As needed, the decision was communicated in writing to other Christians or churches affected by the Jerusalem gathering.

Additional guidelines are discovered in this account. The entire meeting was conducted in a spirit of love, of mutual respect and trust. In other teaching given the church, there is counsel indicating this behavior and attitude is important: "Rebuke not an elder" (1 Timothy 5:1 KJV); be "self controlled"; "love what is good"; be "holy and disciplined"; "encourage others" (Titus 1:8, 9 NIV). "Be devoted to one another in brotherly love"; "honor one another above yourselves"; "practice hospitality"; "live in harmony with one another"; "do not be proud"; "do not be conceited"; "live at peace with everyone"; "do not think of yourself more highly than you ought"; and, "approve what God's will is—his good, pleasing and perfect will." (Rom. 12 NIV) These are the qualities and characteristics that allow a meeting for worship for the conduct of business to proceed harmoniously and effectively. Any breakdown in this pattern can be damaging to the entire church.

It is obvious that only by the grace of God and a learned art of working together can the work of the church be done. This is a method to be learned. It has been said of Friends that in our worship for business sessions, "The least member in the church hath an office and is serviceable and every member hath need one of another." (George Fox's *Journal*) The yearly meeting or larger regional meeting does not exist to exert authority over the smaller groups, nor does a smaller fellowship assume to dominate the larger group. Each is both means and end. The yearly meeting exists largely to widen the range of undertakings too big for the smaller groups. Through it constituent parts provide organization and direction and money to support the enterprises such as colleges, home and foreign missions, youth programs, church extension, social action, publications—any number of efforts only a cooperative effort can attempt. The yearly meeting also "records" ministers, issues credentials to traveling Friends, appoints committees to deal with a variety of issues and concerns beyond the range of the smaller meetings such as testimonies for peace, national legislation, social concerns, evangelism, and publications.

The Apostle Paul once said, "Love does not insist on...its own way." (1 Cor. 13:5 RSV) This is the highest binding force within any religious group and the only real force that will make of us a truly Christian church, church member or leader. God is love. In the Gospel of John we are reminded again that "Greater love hath no man than this, that a man lay down his life for his friends." (John 15:13 KJV)

The Friends Church has been known as a "church of love." If this binding strength of obedience to Christ, the unity of love, and the significance of true worship continues to characterize our fellowship, a spiritual revival of the church is assured.

"Finally, all of you, live in harmony with one another; be sympathetic, love as brothers, be compassionate and humble." (1 Peter 3:8 NIV)

These are more than ideals, they are realities to be experienced.

Chapter VI

ON BEING POWERFUL

*But you shall receive power—ability, efficiency and
might—when the Holy Spirit has come upon you....*
—Acts 1:8 Amplified NT

A re you a "powerful" Christian? Few of us
would say so. We are uncomfortable describing ourselves this way...or anyone else. Yet
this is what Jesus, just before His ascension, said His followers
were to be. "You will receive power when the Holy Spirit
comes on you...." (Acts 1:8 NIV)

Spiritual power is a mysterious and easily misunderstood
thing. Among Friends, to speak of exercising power, even spiritual power, makes us a little edgy, defensive, or downright
afraid. It is too easy to settle for a spiritual or church status
quo, like the Children of Israel going in circles for forty years
in the wilderness. Or, like a dear elder remarked after an
enthusiastic church meeting about goal setting: "But don't you
understand? Friends meetings are always small and struggling!" You see, we can become so stalled, paralyzed, exhausted and disillusioned, or so used to routine religious rat racing
that we really don't let our mind dwell on alternatives. Jesus'
Way is a wonderful *alternative*.

Spiritual power is hard to photograph, even with words. We need models. The Book of Acts, fortunately, is full of them. Remember Peter? We know him pretty well—too well! His track record through the Gospels is like looking in a mirror. It is a wearisome rerun of too many of us. Blustery, boastful, talkative, chairing too many committees, always on center stage, losing his temper, denying, weeping, repenting, *running* to the empty tomb. Then, Peter comes out of the Upper Room on Pentecost Day a different kind of disciple. There is a new solid core in his confidence. Power! *He*, like his Master, became like one speaking with authority—courageous in spite of being prominently placed on the persecutors' hit list, *sleeping* between prison guards instead of swearing at them.

That is powerful! It is the difference between mere human propulsion into church work and the Spirit's uplifting. But, we protect ourselves too carefully from such dreaming, from expecting the impossible. "Expect a Miracle" is a borrowed slogan, but it is something to think about.

Remember that we as filled-with-the-Spirit people are not to be "squeezed into the world's mould" (Rom. 12:1 *Phillips*), which means not molded by materialistic, safety-at-any-cost mentality of the world. The Holy Spirit, the sanctifier, the One who comes in supernatural power to us has *special strength.* Boldness, creativity, confidence, adequacy for Christian living and serving result from His taking over. The greatest feature of our faith is His promise to make us powerful "unto the end." Our hope is in the raw, real power of the Holy Spirit at work among Friends. There is no shortage of future for Christians.

In the Book of Acts, power was promised and it came. The Lord always does just as He promises. "They were filled with the Holy Spirit...and boldness." And, that "filledness" has a special verb form. It means a continuing, ongoing inflow and outgo in direct proportion to being especially equipped for the thing at hand.

It is the work of God, however. One doesn't preach, scold, or shame others into having spiritual power. Nor does it happen from plugging into a theological formula. Hearing that if one is just more committed, or prays more, or works harder he or she will be filled with the Holy Spirit's power brings a sense of weariness. Yet those "ordinary" individuals listed in the Gospel, coming from Galilee, most of whom had no earned degrees or great fame, had power. Even their shadow on the street made a great impact for good.

Being convinced that Friends have convictions based on Truth and that Quaker values are important may still result in a sterile spiritual emptiness. With all the benefits of an impressive past and an exciting future it is still possible to drift into mere religious routine and tradition unless the power flows.

Have you seen the Grand Coulee Dam? Described in a brochure for visitors as the largest engineering feat in history, this huge construction is a powerful project. But the power is not in the massive concrete walls, nor in the churning, cascading water falling over the enormous barrier holding back the reservoir. The power providing electricity and irrigation for millions of acres is the result of harnessing some of these things God has made and allowing them to benefit all the recipients of the great Grand Coulee project. Power is channeling and using the created resources of God.

Yet, power is not synonymous with bigness. All the elements are available regardless of size. The challenge of industry today is to make little things like silicon chips with memory banks too small to see but able to hold libraries of data. It is just as important to be a silicon chip as it is a skyscraper.

The power of God is needed also to put things in perspective. The Holy Spirit creates and renews the attitudes and the forms to express His Truth through the church we believe in. The Christian church, as already stated, is God's creation. It is His chosen vehicle, His way, for each succeeding generation in building the Kingdom of God in practical expressions of His love. Through His power we are to make human attempts in meeting human needs. Though we believe that all of life can be sacramental, we do not regard the patterns in which we organize our lives or our church as unchangeable or sacrosanct. Quakerism is perfectionist in theology in that our hearts may be perfect toward God. But the church is not served nor filled with the already-perfected. It is Henri Nouwen who says, "To grow is to change, and to be perfect is to change often."

We have also described our belief in a universal ministry of all Christians, yet we all have discovered a lot of human error and frailties in the exercise of these ministries. So, we are not demanding greater power from others than we expect of ourselves. Another definition of spiritual power is the influence one has in the lives of others. More, it is a channel through which the influence, wisdom, counsel and callings of the Holy Spirit flow. This means that when this happens our lives bless, uplift, and help all those we touch. This is a sacred thing, but it happens.

This is why this entire study of who we are as Friends is important. Hopefully it will inspire a search for the vision of ourselves, our church and for the world that will guide us. Unless our beliefs inform us, inspire us, move us to action, and give us a joyful satisfaction there will be no energy for effective witness to the Truth.

The early church became a vastly energetic, confident, convincing group, which also describes Quakers when at their best in history. Such vigor and wisdom is to characterize us today! The distinctives defined and described are given not just to make us Quakers, but to show how the Gospel has been demonstrated and is able to fit this generation. It is a call to raise a standard of righteousness, to respond to and live by God's way of truth and love, faith and practice.

Spiritual power is not a human talent skillfully used, but rather, an availability to the guidance of God. It has been said that the only authentic leadership in the Friends Church is divine "followship." Influential Christians, pastors or leaders, are not in any important sense initiators; rather, they are responders to the Holy Spirit. The opposite is also true, when we cease to be Spirit-led, the power is gone, the genius of Christian grace becomes mechanical and shallow.

Finding the answers to our identity as Friends in the Kingdom of God is the beginning of power. And that power brings a deep longing to be useful in life; it is rooted in our religious genes. There is, in fact, no desire more sacred to us than finding fulfillment in a ministry of serving and working. These are essential, not only to spiritual survival, but to meaning in life. What good is a Grand Coulee project if it connects to nothing? If our church is to glorify its Creator and exercise a moral force on society, then it must be connected in our living to the issues of our day. This is another way the power flows.

While we all know there are many powerless people, one still knows there are many more who are sensitive, mature, dedicated Christians with vision and energy to meet the challenge of our time. These are those not only willing but eager to take responsibility in the life and leadership of the church.

It is Robert Greenleaf who insists servant-leadership is not in being either a servant or wielding power, but it is wielding power as a servant. The love of God is powerful. Truth and love struggle with falsehood and selfishness in the world, and in the inner world of each of us. Our relationship with the church and all others in the world about us is largely determined by the kind of projection we have made of our own relationship with God. This brings true self-knowledge, which is the only real basis for self-esteem. If fears, anxieties, and even anger remain in us, festering, and enfeebling us, we will not know spiritual power. Power, truth, and love must meet and be reconciled within our hearts as well as within our church.

The keys to spiritual power and effectiveness are in Paul's word to the Christians in Corinth:

"Love must be sincere. Hate what is evil; cling to what is good. Be devoted to one another in brotherly love. Honor one another above yourselves. Never be lacking in zeal, but keep your spiritual fervor, serving the Lord." (Rom. 12:9-12 NIV)

"And now these three remain: faith, hope and love. But the greatest of these is love." (1 Cor. 13:13 NIV)

ALSO BY OR ABOUT JACK L. WILLCUTS

A Family of Friends

> Jack Willcuts offers ten lessons on Quaker doctrine and practice. These lessons introduce readers to the "family of Friends."

The Sense of the Meeting

> This easy-to-read collection of the editorial writings of Jack Willcuts was edited by his daughter Susan Willcuts Kendall.

The Wit and Wisdom of Jack Willcuts
by Arthur O. Roberts

> Arthur Roberts says, "In joyous memory and in appreciation of his fruitful life and ministry, I provide readers with selections from [Jack's] letters...."

For additional Friends resources contact your Friends bookstore or Barclay Press, 800-962-4014, or order online at www.barclaypress.com.

CPSIA information can be obtained
at www.ICGtesting.com
Printed in the USA
BVHW030025310821
615269BV00006B/43

9 780913 342459